Advance Praise

"Arlene Miller gives us the fastest, easiest keys to grammar. Without her help, I wouldn't know whether I was *laying* or *lying* down the law—and I wouldn't even try to compose a novel." **Ransom Stephens, author of *The God Patent***

"Grammar influences grades, hiring, and promotions. Don't let preventable grammatical, punctuation, and/or word usage mistakes sabotage your hard work. Buy, use, and profit from Arlene Miller's eminently usable *Correct Me If I'm Wrong*." **Erik Kassebaum, M.A., Business and Organizational Security Management and Anthropology; management and research consultant at kassebaum.org**

"This book is a pleasure to read: Not only is the information clear and concise, the book layout makes it very easy to find answers to my grammatical questions. I am a writer, and I find this book indispensible when working on a project. I often refer to Arlene's book for a "quick fix" to my writing questions. The book layout is in alphabetical order, which makes it very easy to reference. Well organized! Excellent resource! Fits my needs! Thank you, Ms. Miller!" **Jeannie Thomas, consultant, educator, and author of *A Caregiver's Winding Road***

"Back in sixth grade when I diagrammed sentences, I might have known that articles are really adjectives, but that, and quite a few other conventions of English grammar, surprised me when I read *Correct Me If I'm Wrong: Getting Your Grammar, Punctuation, and Word Usage Right!* I thought I would look the book over, read a few of the (alphabetically arranged) entries for an idea of the contents. Two hours later, I was hooked on grammar! Arlene Miller's clear prose and copious examples make the book easy to read and understand. If *Correct Me If I'm Wrong* can't teach us when to use *who* and *whom,* nothing can. I'm recommending that my students buy it. The introduction, 'A Short Grammar Refresher,' alone is worth the cover price. The book is a 'must' for anyone who wants to write." **Ana Manwaring, columnist, *Petaluma Post*, creative writing and English as a Second Language teacher, author, and owner of JAM editing**

"What a great, concise grammar book that can be easily understood! I love that it is alphabetized to find exactly what I need. Great for students as well as authors." **Jeane Slone, author of *She Flew Bombers* and *She Built Ships During WW II***

"In grammar, as in mathematics, the simplest explanation is always the best; and if the simplest explanation is also a lot of fun, then you must be reading Arlene Miller's *Correct Me If I'm Wrong*. Ms. Miller provides clear solutions to the bewildering puzzles of sentence and syntax, and her delight in this process reveals the pleasure of creating well-crafted language. *Correct Me If I'm Wrong* turns the struggle of grammar into a cheerful game that the reader is invited to join and enjoy." **John Walker, Ph.D., Principal, St. Vincent de Paul High School, Petaluma CA**

"Just as Miller did in *The Best Little Grammar Book Ever!* she has put together another grammar book that is both informative and a pleasure to read. Oh yes, *Correct Me If I'm Wrong* is also immensely useful! I have become a staunch member of her fan club." **Persia Woolley, author of the *Guinevere Trilogy***

The Best Little Grammar Book Ever!

"Thank you for writing *The Best Little Grammar Book Ever!* I believe it ranks with *The Elements of Style* by Strunk and White." **David D. Watts, Associate Vice President, Major and Planned Gifts, Children's Hospital, Los Angeles, CA**

"I have read a lot of grammar books, but this is the best one!" **Tim Nonn, Ph.D., Writer, community organizer, *Petaluma [CA] Argus-Courier* book reviewer**

"A user-friendly, practical, and immensely helpful book on grammar and usage. This volume should have a place on every writer's shelf. Highly recommended." **Sheldon Siegel, *New York Times* best-selling author of *Judgment Day***

"I recently had the pleasure of getting a peek at *The Best Little Grammar Book Ever!* and it is no exaggeration to say I enjoyed—and learned from—every single page. Arlene Miller uses her extensive experience and exuberant manner to assemble a surprisingly entertaining approach to our challenging language. The *Best Little Grammar Book Ever!* packs a ton of useful points in its brief 132 pages. As a writer and editor myself, I particularly favor the end-of-chapter quizzes. Whether you are well-versed in grammar or perhaps in need of a tune-up, I can't think of a more useful tool on your short list of references." **K. Patrick McDonald, paramedic/consultant/ speaker, author of *America's Dumbest Doctors***

"Succinct and easy to understand. Wish I could have learned English grammar this way! A good resource for anyone pursuing a writing career." **Myrna Ericksen, Showcase Publishers, Sacramento, CA**

"Forget those cumbersome and cryptic writing style guides. At last there's one book that covers the real world grammar challenges that regular, everyday people face! Whether you write business letters, Web copy, marketing pieces, articles, novels, or nonfiction books, this is the resource you need to create readable and correct text. I highly recommend it." **Dawn Josephson, the Master Writing Coach™, author of *Write It Right***

"Love the book! I have already used it in the classroom." **Linda Thompson, special education teacher, 7th grade, Petaluma, CA**

"At last, a book that makes choosing and using correct grammar easy. *The Best Little Grammar Book Ever!* works, and works well. Author Arlene Miller, a teacher, knows that we all have a tough time with *who* and *whom, there* and *their;* she succeeds in guiding us, step by step." **Gary Miller, Alaska Apple Users**

"I did enjoy reading this book, as hard as that might be to believe! There are lots of great tips, and it will be a useful reference when a question comes to mind as I am writing. *The Best Little Grammar Book Ever!* will be on my reference shelf for many years to come!" **Dave Noderer, president of Computerways, Deerfield Beach, FL**

"Excellent book! I put it on the shelf next to my copy of Strunk and White's *The Elements of Style.* There is no extra fluff to wade through. The lessons are quick, simple, and to the point." **Robin Moore, author**

Includes
Expanded Section
on Comma Use

Correct Me ✓
If I'm Wrong

Enjoy!

Getting Your Grammar,
Punctuation, and
Word Usage Right!

Arlene Miller

Arlene Miller

Author of *The Best Little Grammar Book Ever!*

ISBN: 978-0-9843316-3-5
Library of Congress Control Number: 2012910221

Editor: Linda Jay Geldens
Book Designer: Val Sherer
Cover Designer: Matt Hinrichs

Arlene Miller is available for keynote speeches, as well as grammar and business writing workshops. This book is available to schools, libraries, and organizations. For bulk orders and information on presentations and workshops, please contact us.

www.bigwords101.com
nfo@bigwords101.com

To Jake and Shelley,

With Unconditional Love

Contents

Acknowledgments

A book is never the work of one person. I would like to thank the following people for their help in making this book a reality.

I must first thank my writing colleague Marie Millard. Marie sent me a Facebook message one day saying that she had a dream I wrote a book called *Correct Me If I'm Wrong.* So, how could I not?

The Redwood Writers and the Bay Area Independent Publishers Association, two groups to which I belong, have inspired me and helped me from Day One. I couldn't have written one grammar book, let alone two, without their inspiration and help. Thank you to all my friends at those organizations, among them Linda Reid, Pete Masterson, and Joel Friedman.

Thank you, fellow writer Jeane Slone, who distributes local authors' books throughout Sonoma County, California, and has given me many book sales!

Special thanks to Linda Jay Geldens, who edited this book; Val Sherer, who designed the interior; and Matt Hinrichs, who designed the cover.

And thank you, Jeannie Thomas and John DeGaetano, who keep me honest—and hard at work.

–Arlene Miller

How to Use This Book

This book begins with a brief grammar review. After that short refresher, the rest of the book is arranged in alphabetical order. Hopefully, the answer to every grammar, punctuation, and word usage question you have will be easy to find. There is also an appendix of writing "no-no's" and a complete index. You may want to read this book cover to cover—or you may want to use it as a reference book when you have a question.

I have included a detailed section on comma use, since commas are perplexing to most of us!

The book is filled with examples. The word ***example*** is in ***italics*** and **boldface,** so you can easily find all the examples. Words used as themselves (and words to note in the examples) are in ***italics and boldface***.

Please feel free to contact me at info@bigwords101.com (especially if there is something you particularly like or something that you can't find).

Other contact information is included at the end of this book, along with ordering information for this book and my other books.

Introduction:
A Short Grammar Refresher

This is by no means a complete course in grammar, but instead a brief overview of the parts of speech and the structure of sentences.

The Parts of Speech: The Building Blocks

Every word belongs to one or more ***parts of speech***. Parts of speech indicate the word's function, what it does. Here are the parts of speech:

1. **Noun:** Person, place, thing, or idea

   Examples: girl, house, cat, bravery, place, sky, neighbor, Mary, California

2. **Pronoun:** Takes the place of a noun (or another pronoun)

   Examples: he, she, it, our, myself, everyone, this, that, who

3. **Verb:** Action word or state of being

   Examples: jump, run, walk, think, study, are (***are*** is a state-of-being verb)

4. **Adjective:** Describes a noun, pronoun, or another adjective

   Examples: pretty, big, green, tired, intelligent

5. **Adverb:** Describes a verb, adjective, or other adverb

   Examples: quickly, too, very, slowly, shyly, extremely

6. **Preposition:** Used in a phrase to show the relationship between it and a verb or noun

   Examples: in, out, up, down, under, over, between, along, at, to, for, with

7. **Conjunction:** Joins words, phrases, clauses, or sentences

    Examples: and, for, or, nor, but, so, for, because, although, until, whenever

8. **Interjection:** Expresses emotion

    Examples: Oh! Gee! Ouch! Wow! Well!

9. **Articles:** the words *a, an,* and *the*—they are really adjectives

The Simple Sentence

A sentence is a complete thought. All you need to make a sentence is a **subject** and a **verb**. The subject is always a noun or a pronoun. Here are some examples of subjects and verbs, making a complete sentence:

    Examples: The girl (subject) talks (verb).
    He studies.
    We ski.
    The student thinks.

Obviously, most sentences are quite a bit longer than that! There are many things we can add to sentences. We can add **direct objects**. Objects are always nouns or pronouns, just like subjects. However, the subject is usually doing the action of the verb; the object is receiving the action of the verb. If you ask **what** or **who** about the verb, you will find the direct object. Note that not all sentences have a direct object.

    Examples: She plays **chess**. (She plays what? chess)
    He bakes a **cake**. (He bakes what? a cake)
    They read **magazines**. (They read what? magazines)

We can also add **indirect objects,** also nouns or pronouns.

    Examples: She gives **us** cookies.
    He gave **me** the directions.
    Mom baked **me** a cake.

We can add adjectives and adverbs for more interesting sentences.

> **Examples:**   She gives us **chocolate** cookies. (adjective)
>
> He **quickly** gave me directions. (adverb)
>
> Mom baked me a **very pretty** cake. (adverb, adjective)

We can add conjunctions to connect words.

> **Examples:**   Joe **and** Tom gave us cookies.
>
> Joe asked us if we wanted cookies **or** fruit.

If we need excitement, we can use interjections.

> **Examples:**   **Wow!** That's a pretty fish.
>
> **Ouch!** That cut hurts.
>
> **Well,** I didn't know you would be there.

Phrases

Phrases are small groups of related words that we can add to sentences. Phrases can contain nouns or verbs, but they never contain both a subject and a verb. There are several types of phrases.

1. **Prepositional phrases** start with a preposition and end with a noun or pronoun. They often tell where, when, or what kind; they can describe a noun or a verb. Sometimes you can put a prepositional phrase at the beginning of a sentence; other times, the phrase goes near the word it modifies.

   > **Examples:**   We sat **in the kitchen**. (tells where)
   >
   > We ate **after the game**. (tells when)
   >
   > I chose the tie **with stripes**. (tells what kind)
   >
   > **After the movie** we went to dinner. (tells when)

2. **Participial phrases** contain ***participles,*** which are verb forms that serve as adjectives. A present participle ends with ***-ing***; a past participle takes the past tense form of the verb. Because the verb really is no longer a verb, a participle is called a **verbal**.

    Examples: ***Calling out her daughter's name,*** the mother looked all over for her.

    Sitting in my lap, my cat began to purr.

    I took the ***frozen*** fish out of the freezer. (participle with no phrase)

    The girl, ***singing a song,*** skipped down the lane.

3. **Appositive phrases** describe nouns or pronouns that come directly before the phrase.

    Examples: The man, ***my next-door neighbor,*** is on vacation.

    Did you read my book, ***the mystery,*** yet?

4. **Infinitive phrases** contain a verb preceded by the word ***to*** (which is an infinitive) and serve as nouns.

    Examples: Tell her ***to go across the street***.

    To be a doctor is my primary goal.

5. **Gerund phrases** serve as nouns. A gerund is a verb form ending in ***-ing***. It differs from a present participle (which also ends in ***-ing***) because a participle functions as an adjective, and a gerund functions as a noun (and can be a subject or an object, since it is a noun).

    Examples: ***Going skiing in Aspen*** is my favorite vacation. (The phrase is the subject.)

    I love ***swimming in the lake***. (The phrase is the object.)

Clauses

Like phrases, clauses are also groups of related words. However, unlike phrases, clauses have both a subject and a verb. Well, you ask, isn't that a sentence? Yes, sometimes. There are two primary types of clauses: Independent clauses are complete sentences and can stand alone. Dependent (or **subordinate**) clauses are not complete sentences and cannot stand on their own.

>**Examples:**   Independent clause: I play soccer every week.
>
>Dependent clause: Although I play soccer every week. (This is not a complete sentence. What about playing soccer every week? Something is missing here.)

To make a dependent clause into a complete sentence, you need to add an independent clause to it.

>**Example:**   Although I play soccer every week, **I am not very good at it**. (You added a complete sentence to the dependent clause to make it a complete thought.)

In addition to being either dependent or independent, clauses function as either adjectives, adverbs, or nouns. Adjective clauses usually modify a noun in the sentence. Adverb clauses usually modify a verb in the sentence. Noun clauses usually serve as a subject or an object (because that is what nouns do in a sentence).

Adjective clauses start with the words **who, which, whom, whose,** or **that**. You will never find an adjective clause at the beginning of a sentence.

>**Examples:**   This table, **which I purchased at an antique store,** has lasted for 25 years. (This adjective clause describes the table.)
>
>My friend **who is having the party** is moving away soon. (This clause describes my friend.)

Notice that sometimes an adjective clause is set off in commas and sometimes it isn't. Refer to the following sections for more information: "Commas" and *"That, Which,* or *Who?"*

Adverb clauses start with words such as ***although, because, if, until, since, whenever, after,*** and ***before***. These clauses can be anywhere in a sentence, including at the beginning.

> **Examples:** ***Because I was late for my flight,*** I couldn't get on the plane.
>
> ***Although it is Friday,*** I need to work late.
>
> I am sure he will lend you some money ***if you ask him***.

Noun clauses function as the subject or object in a sentence.

> **Examples:** I know ***who you are***. (The clause is the direct object of ***know***.)
>
> ***Where I am going*** is none of your business. (The clause is the subject of the sentence.)

Sentence Structures

Phrases and clauses make your writing more interesting and complex. You don't want to write all your sentences the same way; that would be boring. Therefore, sometimes you start your sentences with the subject and verb. But other times, you may want to begin with a phrase or a clause. Adding phrases and clauses to your sentences adds interesting and necessary details. There are a few different types of sentence structures, and when you write you will want to use them all.

Simple sentences contain just one independent clause. That doesn't mean they are actually simple. They can contain any number of phrases, adjectives, adverbs, conjunctions, etc.

Examples: I play golf.

Every morning my brothers and I play a game of golf at the new country club around the corner.

Both of these are simple sentences, but notice how much longer and more complex the second sentence is.

Compound sentences contain two or more simple sentences (one independent clause each) connected by either a conjunction or a semicolon.

Examples: ***I play soccer*** and ***my sister dances***.

My brother and I play golf every morning, but ***my sister doesn't like golf,*** so ***she stays home with the dogs***.

Send me the bill; I will pay it next week.

Notice that there are still no dependent clauses in those sentences, but only simple sentences (independent clauses) connected with a conjunction or a semicolon.

Complex sentences contain one independent clause and one or more dependent clauses.

Examples: ***Although my brother and I play golf*** (dependent), ***my sister prefers to stay home*** (independent).

My brother, who is a great golfer, always wins the game. (***Who is a great golfer*** is the dependent clause. ***My brother always wins the game*** is the independent clause.)

Compound/complex sentences combine the features of compound and complex sentences: two or more independent clauses (compound) and one or more dependent clauses (complex).

Example: My brother, who is a great golfer, is going with me, and my sister is staying home. (***My brother is going with me, and my sister is staying home*** is compound; ***who is a great golfer*** is a dependent clause, making the sentence also complex.)

Abbreviations and Symbols: Can I Use Them?

In formal writing, it is best to avoid abbreviations, contractions, and symbols. In tables or memos, where the main focus is to get the information across quickly, it is fine to use abbreviations and symbols. Here are some pointers:

- Some things are never spelled out, for example, **mister** and **junior** as part of a person's name. Do make sure you put a period after these abbreviations.

- Always spell a word out if its abbreviation is only a letter or two shorter than the word spelled out.

- If a company uses an abbreviation or symbol in its name, write the name exactly as the company does.

- Most abbreviated words have periods after them: a.m., Inc., e.g.

- Abbreviations containing capital letters (for example, FBI) generally do not have periods.

- College degrees, however, usually do have periods: B.A., M.S., Ph.D.

- Be consistent. If you use an abbreviation, it is usually good to spell it out the first time you use it, with the abbreviation in parentheses. After the first occurrence, just use the abbreviation. Don't abbreviate some instances of the word, and then spell it out in other instances. For example: Future Farmers of America (FFA) for the first usage.

- If you are compiling a table or chart, or writing a memo, and everyone who reads it understands the abbreviations and symbols, you don't need to write them out or explain them.

- Avoid contractions in formal writing. Once again, contractions are okay for memos and informal writing. Some contractions, such as **can't, won't,** and **I'm,** are so common that you can use them, but it is never wrong to avoid them altogether. Definitely stay away from contractions such as **could've** or **would've,** where the word **have** is shortened.

- If you have a choice between using a contraction or an abbreviation, use the abbreviation. Example: **cont.,** not **cont'd,** for **continued**.

Accept or *Except?*

This one isn't too difficult. **Accept** is a verb, an action, meaning to take something. **Except** has to do with leaving out.

Examples: I **accept** the position of chairperson.

Everyone was invited **except** Joe.

Active or Passive Voice?

Voice applies to verbs only—action words. No other part of speech has voice.

In **active voice,** the subject of the sentence is performing the action of the verb. For example: She drove her brother to school. The subject of the sentence **(she)** is actually doing the driving. Thus, the verb is active.

In **passive voice,** the subject of the sentence is not doing anything, but instead is receiving the action. For example: Her brother was driven to school. **Brother** is the subject of the sentence, but he isn't **driving** (the verb). Thus, the verb is passive.

Examples: He **ate** the pizza. (active)

The pizza **was eaten** in five minutes. (passive)

> The president of the club **awarded** the prizes. (active)
>
> She **was given** a special award by the president of the club. (passive)
>
> He **gave** his brother a bicycle for his birthday. (active)
>
> His brother **was given** a bicycle for his birthday. (passive)

When you write, use the active voice most of the time. There are two instances where you might use the passive voice.

First, use the passive voice when you don't know who did it. For example: The school **was built** in 1980. We may not know (or care) who built the school; the important thing is that it was built in 1980.

Second, use the passive voice when you don't care who did it—when the important thing is that it was done, not who did it. For example: She **was awarded** the highest honors at graduation. We don't care who awarded her the honors; the important thing is that she was awarded the honors.

Once again, use the active voice most of the time in your writing. It is more interesting to use active verbs.

Adjectives: Consecutive and Compound

Adjectives are words that describe nouns. For example: blue dress (**blue** is an adjective), pretty flower (**pretty** is an adjective).

Sometimes you need to use punctuation with adjectives.

If you are using two adjectives to describe the same noun, you may need to put a comma between them. For example, instead of saying **old** *dress,* you want to say ***torn, old dress***. ***Torn*** and ***old*** both describe dress, so you would need a comma between them.

However, if one adjective is describing the other adjective, instead of both adjectives describing the noun, there is no comma. For example, in ***bright blue dress, bright*** describes ***blue,*** the other adjective, not ***dress***.

Hint: If you can put the word ***and*** between the two adjectives and it makes sense, you need a comma.

Sometimes you are going to use compound adjectives (two words used together). For example: ***record-breaking*** race, ***spine-tingling*** adventure, or ***well-done*** steak. When you have two words being used together to describe a noun, put a hyphen between them.

However, as often occurs in the English language, there is an exception to this rule! If you are putting the compound adjective **after** the noun, there is generally no hyphen. For example: The race was ***record breaking***. This movie was ***spine tingling***. (With ***well-*** and ***self-,*** you generally use a hyphen anyway.)

Affect or *Effect?*

Yes, this can be a tricky one, but it really isn't that confusing. The difference between the two words is their parts of speech. ***Affect*** is a verb; ***effect*** is a noun. Since ***affect*** is a verb, you can put ***to*** in front of it (***to affect*** something). Since ***effect*** is a noun, you can put ***an*** in front of it (***an effect***).

Examples: The rainy weather ***affects*** my mood. (Used as a verb—an action word.)

The rainy weather has an **effect** on me. (Used as a noun. ***Effect*** is a thing.)

Examples:　I wonder if this test will **affect** my grade.

Do you think this test will have an **effect** on my grade?

Too much sugar can **affect** your health.

Too much fat has a bad **effect** on your health.

Exception? Yes, of course! About 5 percent of the time, these words are used as the opposite part of speech from the usual, but don't worry too much about it.

Examples:　That girl has a strange **affect**. (meaning a strange way of acting)

The president hopes to **effect** change in the club. (meaning to cause)

Agreement: What's That?

Agreement concerns singulars and plurals.

Subject-Verb Agreement

The subject and the verb of your sentences must always agree. If your subject is singular, your verb must also be singular.

What is a singular verb? It is the form you use with **he** or **she**. For example, **she plays**. Now we know that **plays** is the singular form of the verb **play**. To find out the plural form of a verb, use **they** as the subject. **They play**. Therefore, **play** is the plural form of the verb. Notice that verb plurals are the opposite of noun plurals. Usually, the plural form of a noun has an **s** added at the end. However, the plural of a verb is the form without an **s**.

Examples: The ***mayor makes*** a speech every month. (***Mayor*** is singular and ***makes*** is singular.)

The ***boys make*** dinner on Tuesdays. (***Boys*** is plural and ***make*** is plural.)

This is easy enough. However, sometimes the going gets a little tougher:

1.   Two singular subjects joined by ***and*** are now plural and take a plural verb.

Example: The boy **and** the girl **are walking**. (***Are*** is the plural form. You wouldn't say ***is walking***.)

2.   Obviously, two plurals joined by ***and,*** or one plural and one singular joined by ***and,*** will be plural.

Examples: The boys ***and*** the girls ***are*** walking. The boy ***and*** the girls ***are*** walking.

3.   Two singular subjects joined by ***or*** are singular. It is one or the other.

Example: Either John ***or*** Fred ***is*** going. (Either John or Fred ***are*** going is incorrect. ***John or Fred*** is singular, and ***is*** is singular.)

4.   What if you have two subjects joined by ***or,*** and one of the subjects is singular and one is plural? The verb agrees with the subject that is closer to the verb.

Examples: Either the boy ***or*** his sisters ***are*** going with us. (***Are*** is plural and agrees with the closer subject, ***sisters***.)

Either the boys ***or*** the coach ***is*** going with us. (***Is*** is singular and agrees with the closer subject, ***coach,*** which is singular.)

5.   If you have words between your subject and verb, try to ignore them. They don't change the fact that the subject is singular.

Example: The **girl,** along with her brothers, **is going** to the prom. (The subject is still **girl,** and it is singular, agreeing with **is**.)

Collective Nouns

Sometimes you have a noun that looks singular, but represents a plural, for example, **group, class, band, bunch, family, cast, orchestra, troop**. These are called **collective nouns**. Do you use a singular or a plural verb? Most people always use a singular verb with these words, which appear to be singular. However, technically, you should use a singular verb with these nouns if you are talking about the noun as a unit, but a plural verb if you are talking about the noun's individual members.

Examples: The **family is** having a picnic on Sunday. (Here, we use a singular verb, **is,** because the family is all doing something together as a unit.)

My **family are** coming from all over the country for Christmas. (Here, we have used a plural verb because we are talking about the individual family members, who are each coming from a different place. We are not really referring to the family as a unit.)

Most people do not make this distinction in their writing or speaking, so you decide. So many people use the singular verb all the time that when you use the plural verb, it actually sounds wrong (although it isn't).

Pronoun-Antecedent Agreement

Before we go any further with this, we need to make sure we know what **pronouns** and **antecedents** are. A pronoun is a word that takes the place of, or stands in for, a noun.

Examples: Ted is standing over there. (The subject is **Ted,** which is a noun.)

He is standing over there. (Instead of **Ted,** we can use the pronoun **he**.)

The antecedent is the word that the pronoun is standing in for. So, in the example above, **Ted** is the antecedent of the pronoun **he**.

It makes sense that pronouns should agree with their antecedents. They should either both be singular or both plural.

Examples: Ted and Don are standing over there.

They are standing over there. (**They** is plural, standing in for Ted and Don. Notice also that the verb **are standing** is plural. The verb must also agree.)

Ted brought **his** book to class. (**His** is the pronoun. It is standing in for **Ted.**) **His** and **Ted** are both singular and masculine. You wouldn't say **Ted** brought **their** book to class, or **Ted** brought **her** book to class. (Well, you might, because they both make sense, but in those two examples, the pronoun wouldn't be standing in for **Ted.**)

The rules for using **and** and **or** here are the same as for verb agreement (see the beginning of this section).

Examples: **Julie and Myra** brought **their** bathing suits. (Two singulars connected by **and** are plural.)

Either Julie or Myra brought **her** bathing suit. (Two singulars joined by **or** are still singular. Don't use **their** here.)

If you are combining a single and a plural subject with **or,** always put the plural closer to the antecedent; otherwise, the meaning of the sentence may be confusing.

Example: Either the president **or** the committee members **are** bringing their notes to the meeting. (You wouldn't want to say **Either the committee members or the president is bringing his notes to the meeting**.)

You always want to write in a gender-neutral way, so you may need to rewrite if you don't know the gender.

Examples: If a new customer calls you, always remember to get **his** e-mail address.

You are assuming the customer is male. You can always say **his or her,** but that can be a little awkward. Try changing the subject to a plural to avoid the problem.

Example: When new **customers** call, always remember to get **their** e-mail addresses.

Special Problems:

1. **All the girls wore a long dress to the wedding**.

    Did all the girls wear the same long dress?

    How about changing it to

    All the girls wore long dresses to the wedding.

2. Certain pronouns, called **indefinite pronouns,** can pose a problem. Indefinite pronouns include words such as **everyone, anything, no one, none, each,** and **somebody**. All of those words are singular.

Everybody doesn't sound singular, does it? Well, it is, and you can tell by using the word in a sentence. You will probably use a singular verb without thinking.

Examples:	***Everybody is*** going to the party. (***Is*** is a singular verb. You wouldn't say ***Everybody are going to the party***.)
	This can be a problem when you use another pronoun with ***everyone*** or ***everybody***.
Example:	***Everybody*** who ***is*** coming to the party should bring ***his or her*** camera. Since ***his or her*** can be awkward, it is best to rewrite the sentence.
Example:	***Everybody*** who ***is*** coming to the party should bring a camera. Or,
	All people who ***are*** coming to the party should bring ***their*** cameras. (Make the subject plural, and use ***their***.)

All the pronouns that end in ***-thing, -body,*** and ***-one*** are singular. ***(anyone, anybody, anything, nothing, no one, nobody, everyone, everything, everybody, someone, something, and somebody)***

Allusion or *Illusion?*

And while we're at it, ***elude*** or ***allude*** (there is no ***illude***)?

An illusion is something that isn't there; or something deceptive or misleading, causing you to see it one way, when it really is another way.

Example:	It was just an ***illusion*** that I was making more money than I had made last year.

An allusion is a reference to something.

Example:	In his speech he made an ***allusion*** to his childhood.

If you make an allusion, you allude. ***Allude*** is different from ***elude***. To elude means to avoid or escape something.

Example:	He ***eluded*** the police by hiding in a dumpster.

Notice that ***elude*** is the only one of these words with a single ***l***.

Almost or *Most?*

Don't use ***most*** when you mean ***almost***.

> ***Examples:*** Correct: ***Almost*** everyone is going to the museum.
>
> Incorrect: ***Most*** everyone is going to the museum.

Already or *All Ready?*

All ready for this one?

All ready means ready to go.

Already refers to time.

> ***Examples:*** I am ***all ready*** to go.
>
> I ***already*** came home.
>
> The cakes are ***all ready*** to serve.
>
> I ***already*** served the cakes.

Alright or *All Right?*

This one is pretty simple. I am feeling ***all right***. My answers are ***all right***. Is it ***all right*** if I go with you? ***All right***. Come with me.

When do you use ***alright***? Never! It isn't a word. Don't confuse it with ***already,*** which *is* a word.

All Together or *Altogether?*

All together means everyone together. **Altogether** means completely.

Examples: Let's sing **all together** for the finale.

There is **altogether** too much pepper in this sauce.

Among or *Between?*

I am dividing the pie **between** my friend and me. However, I am dividing the pie **among** the three of us.

Use **between** when you are referring to two things.

Use **among** when you are referring to more than two things.

And while we are talking about **between,** please say **"between you and me,"** never **"between you and I."**

And, But, So: Can I Start a Sentence with Them?

And, but, and **so** are conjunctions, used for joining things. Some people start sentences with them.

Examples: **And** how are you?

But never do that.

So, I think I will go shopping.

You can start sentences with these words in casual conversation, but in writing, I wouldn't. It is incorrect, especially if you are writing a business letter or other formal document.

And: Should I Use a Comma Before It?

We are talking here about the Oxford comma, as it is called. It was used first by the Oxford University Press. It is the comma before the ***and*** in a series. For example: ***I want the red, white, and blue shoes***. That sentence uses the Oxford (or series) comma.

I want the red, white and blue shoes. That sentence doesn't use the Oxford comma.

Neither one is incorrect. You can do either. I prefer using the comma, and I always tell my students to use it. It tends to go in and out of fashion. Although I prefer it, you may not. However, once you decide to use it or not—be consistent. Either use it throughout your entire document in all your series, or don't use it in any of your series. That goes for anything that is debatable, or anything you can't find a definite answer for. Be consistent, and you will look as if you know what you are doing.

Antecedents: Are Mine Clear?

What might an **antecedent** be, you ask? Well, a pronoun (such as ***he, she, they, everyone, we***) is a word that stands in for a noun (or sometimes another pronoun). The antecedent is the noun (or pronoun) that the pronoun is standing in for.

Examples: ***Mary*** is my sister. ***She*** is a teacher. (***She*** is standing in for ***Mary***.)

The ***students*** brought ***their*** books with ***them***. (***Their*** is standing in for ***students,*** and ***them*** is also standing in for ***students***.) You could put the word ***students*** where ***their*** and ***them*** are, but it wouldn't sound very good.

Example: The students brought the students' books with the students.

See what I mean?

You want to make sure that your antecedents are clear, meaning you want to make sure your reader knows which word your pronoun is standing in for. The most common pronouns that might be unclear are ***this, which,*** and ***it***. If you write a sentence and then start the next sentence with ***this*** or ***it,*** it may be unclear what ***this*** or ***it*** stands for.

Example: We are having our meeting at the Old Farmhouse on Kerns Road. ***It*** hasn't always been there.

What hasn't always been there? The meeting? The farmhouse? Rewrite your second sentence. For example, ***Our meetings have not always been held there***.

Any pronoun in a sentence or stuck somewhere in a paragraph can be unclear:

Examples: Unclear: Bob and Jim were hiking when ***he*** fell. (Who fell?)

Bob and Jim were hiking an advanced trail. This was unusual because they were beginning hikers. It doesn't happen very often.

Rewrite: Bob and Jim were hiking an advanced trail. Because they were beginning hikers, they usually stayed off the advanced paths. They don't hike very often.

Unclear: Bob and Jim were hiking an advanced trail when Bob fell, which was unusual. (What was unusual? That Bob fell or that they were hiking an advanced trail?)

Rewrite: Bob and Jim were hiking an advanced trail when Bob fell. They usually hiked the beginning trails because they were inexperienced hikers.

Anymore or *Any More?*

Anymore means at present or now.

Any more means additional.

> **Examples:** We can't find these old-fashioned candy bars **anymore**.
>
> Do you want **any more** dessert?

Anymore is used with a **negative construction**: We can't find these **anymore**.

Avoid using **anymore** with a positive construction: It is hard to find those **anymore**. That bakery has the best doughnuts **anymore**. (Huh??)

Anyone or *Any One?*

Anyone means the same as **anybody**.

Any one means a single one or a single person.

> **Examples:** I can't find **anyone** to unlock the gate.
>
> **Any one** of you can unlock this gate.

Notice that there is a difference between how you pronounce these two words. You are likely to leave a pause between **any** and **one** when **any one** is the correct choice.

As If or *Like?*

Sometimes **like** is used when **as if** should be used.

Correct use of **like**: I feel like a princess.

Incorrect use of **like**: I feel like I am a princess.

The two sentences above are different. The first is correct, but the second sentence should say **I feel as if I am a princess**.

What is the difference? **Like** is used for a simple comparison. In this case we are comparing **I** (whoever **I** is) to **a princess**. The **like** is connecting a pronoun (**I**) and a noun (**princess**).

However, the second sentence has a whole sentence after the word **like** (I am a princess). In this case, you need to use **as if**. **As if** introduces a group of words that has a verb in it (**am,** in this case). Sometimes, instead of **as if,** just use **as**. You will be able to tell the difference, because **as if** will sound wrong.

> **Examples:**   He throws **like** a girl.
>
> He throws **as if** he is a girl.
>
> This tastes **like** New York pizza.
>
> This tastes **as** New York pizza should.

Notice two things about that last example. First, **as if** would sound entirely wrong, so we use **as**. Second, the verb isn't really there, but we can fill it in; it is understood. The sentence really says **This tastes as New York pizza should taste**.

Assure, Ensure, or Insure?

These are all verbs, similar in meaning, but not exactly the same.

Insure usually has to do with making sure of something by protecting it with money.

> **Example:**   I will **insure** my house for $500,000.
>
> I will take out a life **insurance** policy to protect my kids in case I die.

Assure usually has to do with making someone feel confident about something.

> ***Example:***   I ***assure*** you that you will be fine on your plane trip.
>
> She needed extra ***assurance*** to feel safe about her plane trip.

Ensure means to make sure.

> ***Example:***   I will ***ensure*** that the car is safe for you to drive. (There is no ***ensurance***.)

Because Of or *Due To?*

Because of tells why.

Due to is usually used after some form of the verb ***to be***. (***am, is, are***, etc.)

> ***Examples:***   I am late ***because of*** a traffic jam. (I am late because…)
>
> ***Because of*** the weather, I am moving to a different climate. (I am moving because…)
>
> My tardiness is ***due to*** the traffic.
>
> My good grades are ***due to*** hard work.

Because: Can I Start a Sentence with It?

Yes, you can! You may have learned way back in elementary school that you cannot start a sentence with ***because***. This is not true. However, you were taught this for a good reason. Sometimes, especially if you are a young and inexperienced writer, you will start a sentence with **because,** and you will not finish the sentence or thought, thereby ending up with a sentence fragment.

Because I didn't study for the test. This is a sentence fragment and not a complete thought. In grammar, it is known as a dependent clause. You actually need to add an entire sentence to this clause to make it a sentence.

Because I didn't study for the test, I didn't do very well. Now you have a sentence. Notice that you added a complete sentence to your clause: **I didn't do very well** can stand on its own. Notice also that you put a comma after the clause and before the main part of the sentence. You can usually turn this type of sentence around without changing the meaning: **I didn't do very well because I didn't study for the test**. (When **because** is used in the end part of the sentence, there is no comma.)

Bring or *Take?*

These two words are not interchangeable. They go in different directions. You **bring** toward and you **take** away.

Examples: Please **bring** these books home after your friend sees them.

Please **take** these books back to the library.

She is **bringing** a cake to my party.

I am **taking** a cake to my neighbor's party.

By Accident or *On Accident?*

I don't know who started saying **on accident** instead of **by accident** (I thought it might have been my own kids, but I guess not!).

Suffice it to say that **on accident** is just plain wrong. **By accident** is correct.

> **Examples:** I threw the book away **by accident**.
>
> **By accident,** I stepped on my dog.

Capital or *Capitol?*

The correct way to spell this word is usually **capital** with an **-al** at the end. The only **Capitol** with an **-ol** at the end starts with a capital **C** and refers to the building where Congress meets in Washington, D.C. (there was also a Capitol in ancient Rome).

Capitalize? Or Not?

Most of us know the basic rules of capitalization. Here are some of the more tricky ones:

1. Capitalize expressions that are used as sentences.

    > **Examples:** Really?
    >
    > No harm done.

2. Do not capitalize after a colon if the words following the colon are not a complete sentence, or if the sentence following the colon explains or enlarges upon the sentence before the colon.

Example: Do not bring a sweater: *it* is going to be 100 degrees in Boston.

3. Capitalize nouns that are part of a name.

Examples: Tomorrow evening the *mayor* will make a speech.

Tomorrow evening *Mayor Jones* will make a speech.

I heard that the *president* of the company, Mike Greene, was just promoted.

I heard that *President Greene* was just promoted.

There is a game at the *high school* this afternoon.

There is a game at *Wilson High School* this afternoon.

4. Capitalize family members' names if they are being used as a name, rather than as a relationship.

Examples: I can't believe that my *mother* has been baking all day.

I can't believe that *Mother* has been baking all day.

We are going to visit my *grandmother* today.

We are going to visit *Grandmother* today.

We are going to visit *Grandmother Sparks* today.

5. Capitalize *North, South, East,* and *West* when they are areas rather than directions. Capitalize other names that apply to areas as well.

Examples: I have always lived in the *South*.

Turn *south* when you get to Main Street.

My relatives live in the *Bible Belt*.

I have always wanted to travel to the *West*.

6. Capitalize the names of days of the week, months of the year, and holidays. Do not, however, capitalize the seasons (**winter, spring, summer,** and **fall**) unless they are part of a proper noun.

   Examples: I love the **spring**.

                     We are going to the **Spring Festival**.

7. Capitalize the names of specific school courses, but not general subjects.

   Examples: geometry, Geometry II, history, History of England, psychology, Psychology 101

8. Names of products are capitalized, but not the common noun that follows them.

   Examples: Kleenex tissues

                     Campbell's soup

                     Apple computer

9. Capitalize a noun that is followed by a number or letter if sequence is indicated. However, the words **page, line, paragraph, step,** and **verse** are not capitalized.

   Examples: Please turn to **page 158** in your handbook.

                     Go to **Building 5** for your appointment.

                     The answer is in **Chapter 6**.

                     Refer to **step 8** to disassemble the product.

Cite, Sight, or *Site?*

These three words are all pronounced the same, but they have three very different meanings.

Sight has to do with seeing: The Grand Canyon is quite a **sight** to see.

Site is a place: That is the **site** of the new mall. (where it will be built)

Cite is to mention or reference something: In her speech, she **cited** a new book by her brother.

Climactic or *Climatic?*

Climactic has to do with **climax**.

Climatic has to do with **climate**.

> **Examples:** The **climactic** point of this book was really scary!
>
> I have noticed **climatic** changes in the past few years. It has been getting much cooler.

Cloths or *Clothes?*

Cloths are what you wash your car with.

Clothes are what you wear.

> **Examples:** Do you have any spare dusting **cloths**?
>
> I need some new **clothes** for my cruise.

Colon or No Colon in a List?

The main use of the colon (:) is to introduce a list. This list can be either horizontal or vertical.

Here is a vertical list introduced by a colon:

- Ha!

- This is one!

- See the colon!

Here is a horizontal list introduced by a colon: ha, this is one, and see the colon.

Often the word **following** or the phrase **as follows** is used in the introduction to the list, but it doesn't need to be there.

If your introduction to the list is a complete sentence after which you stop, then use a colon. However, if your introduction to the list is not a complete sentence, or if the items in the series complete the sentence that begins in the introduction, do not punctuate it at all.

Examples: The recipe calls for these ingredients: sugar, flour, eggs, milk, and chocolate.

The recipe contains the following ingredients: sugar, flour, eggs, milk, and chocolate.

The recipe contains sugar, flour, eggs, milk, and chocolate.

Note that the last example doesn't use a colon because the sentence flows as it is. You wouldn't want to interrupt the flow by using a colon after **contains**.

Vertical lists work the same way.

The recipe contains the following ingredients:

- sugar

- flour

- eggs

- milk

- chocolate

The recipe contains

- sugar

- flour

- eggs

- milk

- chocolate

It is not awful if you put a colon after the introduction to that second vertical list because there is already a break, since you are now going on to the next line. But leaving the colon out is best.

While we are on the subject of lists, do we need those bullets? No, you could just indent, or not indent at all. What about numbers? Numbered lists usually indicate that either the order matters (as in numbered steps) or that the total number is important (if there are three ways to do something, you would probably want to number the list from one to three).

Since the items in the list are completing the introductory words in that second vertical list, this is also correct:

The recipe contains

sugar,
flour,
eggs,
milk, and
chocolate.

(Yes, you could use bullets too.)

It is never appropriate to use a semicolon here instead of a colon. A semicolon has entirely different uses. It is possible to use a period rather than a colon, but why would you? Use a colon to introduce a list when appropriate.

Comma or Semicolon?

The comma has about 752 rules, as you will see in the next section! On the other hand, the semicolon (;) has only two main uses. Commas and semicolons are **not** interchangeable.

In Compound Sentences

A comma cannot separate two complete sentences unless you use a conjunction (**and, but, or, nor, for, so, yet**) between them. Let me repeat that: **A comma cannot separate two sentences unless you use a conjunction between them**. (Note that the word **then** is not a conjunction and cannot separate two sentences; neither can **however** or **therefore**.)

You can, however, separate two complete sentences with a semicolon if the two sentences are closely related.

> **Examples:** I went to the movies; my sister chose to go to the party. Correct. (no capital letter after the semicolon)
>
> I went to the movies, but my sister chose to go to the party. Correct. (use of conjunction)
>
> I went to the movies. My sister chose to go to the party. Correct. You can always make your sentence two separate sentences and use a period between them.
>
> **More Examples:** I went to the movies, my sister chose to go to the dance. Incorrect. (Don't you dare!)
>
> I went to the movies, however, my sister chose to go to the dance. Incorrect.
>
> I went to the movies, then I went to dinner with my sister. Incorrect.
>
> I went to the movies, therefore, I didn't go to the party. Incorrect.

And More Examples: I went to the movies; however, my sister chose to go to the dance. Correct.

I went to the movies; then I went to dinner with my sister. Correct.

I went to the movies; therefore, I didn't go to the party. Correct.

I went to the movies, ***and*** then I went to dinner with my sister. Correct. (conjunction ***and*** added)

Notice that in the above examples, there is a complete sentence on each side of ***however, then,*** and ***therefore***. You need a semicolon to separate those sentences. You could, of course, also use a period, but a comma is **not** enough.

In a Series

When you have a complicated series that already has commas within it, you will probably want to use semicolons to clarify (or you will want to rewrite). You may also want to use a semicolon for clarity in a compound sentence where there are series in each part. Look at the following examples.

Examples: 1.   Mr. Greene, the department manager, Ms. Trin, Ms. Layton, an engineer, Mr. Gould, the mayor, and Mr. Thomas attended the meeting.

It is nearly (if not completely) impossible to figure out how many people are in that list. We can't really tell if Ms. Layton is the same person as the engineer, or if they are two separate people. The same is true of Mr. Greene (is he the department manager?) and Mr. Gould (is he the mayor?). If we use semicolons between the names, everything becomes much clearer:

Mr. Greene, the department manager; Ms. Trin; Ms. Layton, an engineer; Mr. Gould; the mayor; and Mr. Thomas attended the meeting.

Now, we can tell that Mr. Greene is the department manager, and Ms. Layton is an engineer, but Mr. Gould is not the mayor. There are clearly six people in the list.

Examples: 2. Boston, Massachusetts, Chicago, Illinois, and Los Angeles, California are big cities and Danvers, Massachusetts, Napa, California, and Jupiter, Florida are smaller towns.

You could probably figure out that sentence, but semicolons might make it easier:

Boston, Massachusetts; Chicago, Illinois; and Los Angeles, California are big cities; and Danvers, Massachusetts; Napa, California; and Jupiter, Florida are smaller towns.

Commas:
To Comma or Not to Comma?
That Is the Question

Commas are probably the most confusing aspect of writing. Sometimes it is necessary to use a comma. At other times it is necessary **not** to use a comma. At still other times, it is up to you. Some types of commas go in and out of style (for example, the Oxford, or series, comma). Sometimes a comma will be necessary in a business letter, but could be skipped in a novel. The important thing to remember is that there are rules for using commas. Commas are not to be sprinkled throughout your writing like salt or pepper!

There are many comma rules, some more common than others. I have decided to put most of those rules into this book, so if you are wondering whether or not to use a comma, you will find the answer here!

Here Are Places Where You Need a Comma

1. Use a comma after each item in a series, whether the items are words, phrases, or complete sentences.

   Examples: I brought cheese, bread, juice, and brownies. (words)

                         He went to the mall, to the cleaners, out to lunch, and then to the movies. (phrases)

                         Please clean your room, go to the post office, and do the grocery shopping. (sentences)

                         Notice that I used a comma before the ***and*** in each of the examples. This final comma is called the Oxford comma and has been the subject of much debate. It is up to you whether you choose to use it, but I like it, and I always use it. Whichever way you decide to punctuate your series, be consistent. Either use the Oxford comma, or don't.

2. Use a comma before the conjunction in compound sentences (two or more complete sentences joined by a conjunction like ***and, but,*** or ***so***).

   Examples: I live in Texas, and my brother lives in Utah.

                         I would love to go, but I don't have any money.

If the second part of the sentence is not a complete sentence, do not use a comma (unless the conjunction is ***but;*** see comma rule 28).

   Example: I am shorter than my brother and taller than my sister. (***taller than my sister*** is not a complete sentence, so no comma is used.)

Note that **then** is not a conjunction and cannot be used to separate two sentences unless you use a conjunction with it, or you use a semicolon.

> **Examples:** My sister went to the mall, **then** she came home. (Incorrect)
>
> My sister went to the mall, **and then** she came home. (Correct)
>
> My sister went to the mall; **then** she came home. (Correct)

3. Use a comma between two adjectives that both describe the same noun if you can put **and** between the two adjectives, and it makes sense.

> **Examples:** The dress had a **large, noticeable** stain. (**Large and noticeable stain** makes sense.)
>
> She wore a **bright blue** dress. (Here, there is no comma because **bright** describes **blue**, rather than **dress**. You wouldn't say **bright and blue dress**.)

4. Use commas to set off a word, phrase, or clause that interrupts a sentence with nonessential information. To ensure that you put the commas in the right place, read the sentence leaving out the words between the commas; make sure the sentence makes sense.

> **Examples:** My husband, **John,** is on a business trip. (one-word interrupter)
>
> Mike, **my former boss,** is on a business trip. (phrase interrupter)
>
> Mike, **who is my former boss,** is on a business trip. (clause interrupter)

5. Use a comma to enclose nonessential expressions in the middle of a sentence, and before or after such an expression at the beginning or end of a sentence.

Examples:	That movie, ***in my opinion,*** is not worth seeing.
	In my opinion, that movie is not worth seeing.
	That movie is not worth seeing, ***in my opinion***.

6. Use a comma after an introductory prepositional phrase, especially if it is long or there are two phrases in a row. If the prepositional phrase is short, no comma is necessary, but it is not incorrect to use one.

Examples:	***In Paris*** we saw the Eiffel Tower. (***In Paris*** is a short phrase, so the comma is not necessary.)
	On top of the refrigerator, there was a mouse. (Here, there are two prepositional phrases in a row, ***on top*** and ***of the refrigerator***. Of course, you could always put those phrases at the end of the sentence and avoid the commas.)
	Across the blazing pink sky, the hot air balloon sparkled. (long prepositional phrase)

Note that if the phrase isn't introductory, but is instead followed directly by a verb, there is no comma (On top of the refrigerator ***was*** a mouse. Across the blazing pink sky ***flew*** the hot air balloon.)

Always use a comma after an introductory prepositional phrase that is a comment or transition.

Examples:	***In my opinion,*** there is no solution to this problem. (comment)
	At first, I didn't think we could find a solution. (transition)

7. Use a comma after an introductory participial phrase. An introductory participial phrase should modify, or describe, the subject, which should immediately follow the comma.

Examples: ***Looking left and right, she*** crossed the street.

Reading by the window, I enjoyed the bright sunlight.

Make sure you put the word that the phrase describes right after the comma. Otherwise, you will have a misplaced modifier, like this: ***Reading by the window, the cat*** jumped into my lap. (Since the cat was probably not reading by the window, the sentence has a misplaced modifier and is silly.)

Note that if the phrase is directly followed by a verb, there is no comma. (***Reading by the window relaxes*** me.)

8. Use a comma after an introductory infinitive phrase.

Examples: ***To be a doctor,*** you must go to school for many years.

To get a driver's license, you need to take a written test and a road test.

Note that if the phrase is directly followed by a verb, there is no comma. (***To be a doctor is*** my greatest ambition.)

9. Use a comma after an introductory clause. These clauses usually begin with words like ***because, although, until, since, if, whenever, whatever, before,*** and ***after***.

Examples: ***Because I have so much work to do,*** I cannot go shopping with you.

Although the party sounds like fun, I have a meeting.

If you go to the grocery store, please buy me some sugar.

Whenever she comes to visit, we go sightseeing.

Before you go to the game, call your sister.

Notice that in the examples above, you can switch the sentences around, putting the clauses at the end. If you do that, there is often no comma because the clause is necessary information.

Examples: I cannot go shopping with you because I have so much work to do.

Call your sister before you go to the game.

We go sightseeing whenever she comes to visit.

Please buy me some sugar if you go to the grocery store.

I have a meeting, although the party sounds like fun.

Notice that you would put a comma in the last example because the two parts of the sentence are really not connected; they are not cause and effect.

10. Use a comma after **etc.,** if you are using it in the middle of a sentence.

Example: Take a coat, gloves, scarf, etc., with you when you go to Boston.

11. Use a comma before an afterthought at the end of a sentence.

Examples: Don't wipe your feet on the carpet, **please**.

They sell chocolate doughnuts, **don't they**?

You have been there before, **haven't you**?

12. Use a comma when you are writing dates. However, if you write just the month and year, there is no comma. Look carefully at these different examples.

Examples: March 15, 2012

March 2012

I was born on **March 12, 1985,** in Wisconsin. (Use a comma even after the year if the day is included.)

I was born in **March 1985** in Wisconsin. (No commas are needed if no day is given.)

The **April 2000** issue of **Poetry** magazine includes my poem.

The **April 15, 2000,** issue of **Poetry** magazine is over here. (Needs a comma even after the year because the date is used.)

On **April 15, 2002,** I graduated from the program.

In **April 2002** I graduated from the program. (No comma is needed because the date isn't used, and the phrase is a short introductory phrase.)

Last week, **on May 30,** there was a fire on my street. (Use commas here because **on May 30** interrupts the flow of the sentence.)

May 1, 2008, is a day I will always remember. (Because the date is used, use a comma after the year even though the date is followed by a verb.)

May 2000 is a month I will always remember.

On March 11, 95 people in my company celebrated a birthday. (This comma avoids confusion between the two numbers.)

13. Use a comma in numbers of 1,000 or more.

14. Use a comma to set off descriptive elements.

    Example: The sun, **a huge ball of fire at sunset,** gave the room a beautiful glow.

15. Use a comma after introductory elements in a sentence.

    Examples: **Yes,** I am going with you.

    No, you cannot have any cake.

    In my opinion, you were wrong in this case.

Remember, you need to finish cleaning your room.

Well, I didn't know about that.

Oh, that's fine with me.

16. Use a comma to clarify a sentence with unusual word order.

Examples: Why you didn't tell me, I will never know. (**I will never know why you didn't tell me** is the usual order.)

When you will stop picking on your brother, I can't even begin to figure out. (**I can't even begin to figure out when you will stop picking on your brother** is the usual order.)

17. Use a comma to set off an interrupter within an introductory clause.

Examples: If, **however,** you cannot go, we will ask someone else.

Although, **in my opinion,** that is not a good idea, I will go along with it.

18. Use a comma around any words that interrupt the flow of the sentence.

Examples: Return the book, **whenever you find it,** to your teacher.

I bought that cake, **unhealthy as it might be,** to serve for dessert.

19. Use a comma to set off transitional expressions.

Examples: He is, **additionally,** my second cousin.

Drive, **first,** to the big intersection.

Next, drive to the big intersection.

20. Use a comma to avoid confusion between numbers.

    Example: In our large family of 15, 11 are girls.

21. Use a comma to set off the word **too** in the middle of a sentence, but not before **too** at the end of the sentence.

    Examples: I, **too,** voted for Mike for class president.

    My sons have blond hair **too**.

Note that when **too** means **overly** instead of **also,** you do not use a comma.

    Example: I am **too** tired to go with you.

22. Use a comma in direct address, regardless of where the name is in the sentence.

    Examples: **Mary,** did you ask to speak with me?

    Did you ask to speak with me, **Mary**?

    Did you ask, **Mary,** to speak with me? (Notice how leaving the commas out here would change the meaning of the sentence.)

23. Use commas in direct address that also includes introductory elements or interrupters.

    Examples: **Yes, George,** we will be on vacation next week.

    In my opinion, Joe, we will have to wait until Friday.

    No, Nancy, I didn't go to the movie last night.

24. Use a comma if **or** starts an explanation in a sentence, but not when it represents a choice.

    Examples: He is going to be the drum major, **or lead the marching band**. (explanation)

    He is either going to be drum major **or** a drummer. (choice)

He is taking French I, ***or the introductory course,*** this year. (explanation)

Are you taking French I ***or*** French II next year? (choice)

25. Use a comma to set off academic degrees.

Examples: Joanne Cloud, ***Ph.D.,*** will speak at the graduation.

Joe Clark, ***M.A.,*** is designing my website.

Myra Henry, ***M.B.A.,*** is company president.

26. Use commas to set off ***i.e.*** (that is) and ***e.g.*** (for example) if they are used within a sentence.

Examples: I am going to be the leader, ***i.e.,*** chairperson, of the committee.

She has many farm animals, ***e.g.,*** pigs, sheep, and cows, on her ranch.

27. Use commas in addresses. On an envelope the only comma you need is between city and state. If you are writing an address within text, you will need more punctuation.

Examples: She lives at 35 Baker Street, Miami, Fl 33133.

His address is 10 Main Ave., Taylor, PA 20067.

Note that if you abbreviate the words ***Street, Avenue,*** etc., you need both a period and a comma. Note also that there is never a comma between the state and the zip code.

28. Use a comma in contrasting expressions, usually beginning with ***but, not,*** or ***rather than***.

Examples: I like pizza, ***but*** not with anchovies.

We are going to the movies, ***not*** to the mall.

Pizza, ***rather than*** pasta, will be served at the party.

29. Use commas in company names if the company uses them. In general, write a company's name just as the company writes it, using whatever symbols and punctuation it uses.

   Examples: Geary, Bruner and Shultz (no comma before **and**)

   Paul & Paul Inc.

30. Use a comma to make a sentence clear if a word is left out.

   Examples: The truth is, we don't know the answer. (The word **that** is understood.)

   The fact of the matter is, they have never gotten along.

   We know, not all neighbors are friendly.

However, in most sentences where **that** is left out (and understood), the sentence is perfectly clear, and no comma is needed:

   Examples: I know that she is coming for dinner.

   I know she is coming for dinner. (also clear)

   The book that I borrowed from the library is on the table.

   The book I borrowed from the library is on the table. (also clear)

31. Use a comma in expressions with contrasting elements.

   Examples: Here today, gone tomorrow.

   Garbage in, garbage out.

   Easy come, easy go.

32. You can set off a word in commas for emphasis. (It is not necessary, though.)

   Examples: I agree, **completely,** with everything you said.

   The shy girl spoke, **loudly,** into the microphone.

33. Use a comma after the greeting, or salutation, in a friendly letter. However, use a colon after the salutation in a business letter.

Examples: Dear Susan,

Dear Dr. Jones:

34. Use a comma after the closing of any letter. (Capitalize only the first word of the closing.)

Examples: Yours truly,

Sincerely,

With warm regards,

35. Use a comma to set off the words **however** and **therefore**— sometimes. If the words on each side of **therefore** or **however** are both complete sentences, you cannot simply set those words off with commas. You will need a period or semicolon to avoid a run-on sentence.

Examples: Correct: I don't like the blue suit. The black suit, **however,** fits you well. (Here, **however** is an interrupter, and the sentence makes sense if you leave it out.)

Incorrect: I don't like the blue suit, **however,** the black one fits you very well. (If you take **however** out here, you have a run-on sentence.)

Correct: I don't like the blue suit. **However,** the black one fits you very well.

Correct: I don't like the blue suit; **however,** the black one fits you very well.

Correct: I don't like the blue suit. I think, **therefore,** you should wear the black one. (Here, **therefore** is an interrupter, and the sentence makes sense if you leave it out.)

Incorrect: I don't like the blue suit, **therefore,** I think you should wear the black one. (If you take **therefore** out here, you have a run-on sentence.)

Correct: I don't like the blue suit. **Therefore,** I think you should wear the black one.

Correct: I don't like the blue suit; **therefore,** I think you should wear the black one.

Note that if you add a conjunction like **and** before **therefore,** you can use only commas.

Example: I don't like the blue suit, and, therefore, I think you should wear the black one.

36. Use a comma whenever not using one would cause the reader confusion.

Examples: Correct: As we ate, ants crawled all over our blanket.

Confusing: As we ate ants crawled all over our blanket.

Correct: One dress is red and blue, and the other is green and pink.

Confusing: One dress is red and blue and the other is green and pink.

Correct: The boys belong to the band, and the girls to the chorus,

Confusing: The boys belong to the band and the girls to the chorus.

Correct: The dogs were divided into toy and terrier, and hunter and herder.

Confusing: The dogs were divided into toy and terrier and hunter and herder.

Here Are Places Where You Don't Use a Comma

1. Do not use a comma before a conjunction like **and** or **or** if the words that follow are not a complete sentence (except before **and** in a series.)

    Examples: I washed the dishes and **swept the floors**. **(Swept the floors** is not a complete sentence.)

    Would you like pizza or **chicken**? (Chicken is not a complete sentence, and two items do not make a series.)

    Would you like **pizza, pasta, or chicken**? (Now you have a series, and you can use the comma.)

The conjunction **but** is an exception; you can use a comma before **but** when the words on either side of the conjunction contrast.

    Examples: She is tiny, **but** strong.

    He took the sofa, **but** left the chairs and table.

2. Do not use a comma before or after parentheses unless the sentence would have a comma there anyway.

    Examples: Correct: The company president (he is my cousin) offered me a job.

    Incorrect: The company president, (he is my cousin) offered me a job.

    Incorrect: The company president (he is my cousin), offered me a job.

    Correct: Although he is my cousin (the company president), I think I would have gotten the job anyway. (If you left out what is in parentheses, there would still be a comma.)

3. You do not need a comma after **Jr.** or **Sr.** or **Esq.** in a name.

    Example: Martin Luther King, Jr. is a well-known American.

4. **Never** put a comma between a subject and its verb unless there is an interrupter set off with commas between them.

   Examples: Incorrect: Hannah and her brothers, went to Paris last week.

       Incorrect: The bright blue dress, is in the closet.

       Correct: Hannah and her brothers, who are my cousins, went to Paris last week.

5. **Never** put a comma between a verb and its object.

   Examples: Incorrect: He threw, the ball into the window.

       Incorrect: He is baking, a cake and brownies.

6. **Never** put a comma between an adjective and the noun it modifies.

   Examples: Incorrect: She wore a pretty, dress to the party.

       Incorrect: It was a huge, airplane.

7. **Never** put a comma between a noun or verb and the prepositional phrase that immediately follows it.

   Examples: Incorrect: She was making cookies, in the kitchen.

       Incorrect: There are football fields, tennis courts, and a swimming pool, at the new school. (There should be no comma after **pool**.)

8. Sometimes (see rule 36 above) you use a comma to avoid confusion. However, sometimes putting in a comma **causes** confusion, so you leave it out.

   Example: Richard, my boss, and I are taking a break.

In this sentence we can't tell if the writer is talking about two or three people. Is Richard my boss? We can't tell. It is best to just rewrite such a confusing sentence.

Correct: Richard, who is my boss, and I are taking a break. (two people)

Correct: I am taking a break with Richard and my boss. (three people)

A Few Helpful Notes:

1.   Sometimes you have a choice of whether or not to use a comma.

    Examples: Of course, I will go with you.

                             Of course I will go with you.

2.   If you are setting something off with commas, make sure you have your commas in the correct place. To check, read the sentence without the words within the commas. If it makes sense, you are okay. (Incidentally, the same rule applies for words set off by dashes.)

    Examples: Correct: This car is as good as, but not better than, my old one.

                             Incorrect: This car is as good as, but not better, than my old one. (**This car is as good as than my old one** doesn't make sense.)

3.   Here are some examples of necessary versus unnecessary information in a sentence. Where there are no commas, the words are necessary to the meaning of the sentence. Words that are set off with commas are not necessary to the meaning of the sentence and could be left out without affecting the meaning.

    Examples: 1.   The word *haughty* means snobbish.

                             This word, taken from the French, means *to hurry*.

                         2.   The writer S.E. Hinton wrote *The Outsiders*.

                             The writer, a friend of mine, wrote many poetry books.

                         3.   The book *Gone with the Wind* has been read by millions of people.

The book, which is due at the library, is one of my favorites.

4. My brother Joe went to play golf. (You have more than one brother, so you need to identify him by name.)

My brother, Joe, went to play golf. (He is your only brother, or the reader knows whom you are talking about, so you don't need to name him.)

*Just one more thing: If you **really** cannot find a rule for a comma you are unsure about, read the passage out loud. Then read it again. If the sentence is clear without a comma, leave the comma out.

And now we are done with commas. I promise.

Comparison Gone Wrong?

Sometimes a well-intentioned comparison can be confusing: **She likes pizza more than me**.

Does that mean she likes pizza more than she likes you? Or does she like pizza more than you do? The sentence probably means that she likes pizza better than you like pizza, but it says that she likes pizza more than she likes you. Keep the missing or assumed words in mind (or include them in the sentence) if you want to be sure that you convey the right meaning.

If you say, **She likes pizza more than I like pizza,** or, **She likes pizza more than I do,** now your comparison is clear. Notice also that **I** is correct at the end of that sentence rather than **me**. So saying **She likes pizza more than I** is enough to make it clear.

She likes pizza more than she likes me is the other way the sentence can be taken. In this case, it is correct to use **me**. **She likes pizza more than me** means that she likes pizza more than she likes me.

Comparison: *-Er* or *-Est?*

The **-er** ending on an adjective (for example, **taller**) is called the **comparative**. It is used to compare two things. The **-est** ending on an adjective (for example, **tallest**) is called the **superlative**. It is used to compare more than two things.

> **Examples:**   She is **taller** than her brother.
>
> He is the **tallest** of the three brothers.

If there is no **-er** or **-est** form for that particular adjective (for example, **fun**), use **more** and **most**.

> **Examples:**   This ride was **more fun** than that one. (No, there is no **funner**!)
>
> The roller coaster was the **most fun** of all the rides.

To indicate the opposite direction, always use **less** and **least**.

> **Examples:**   This dress is **less pretty** than that one.
>
> This dress is the **least pretty** of all.

Complement or *Compliment?*

To **compliment** is to say something nice to someone.

To **complement** is to go well with, or to finish nicely.

> **Examples:**   She **complimented** me on my new suit.
>
> He gave me a nice **compliment** on my dress. (used as a noun)
>
> This red wine **complements** the meal nicely.
>
> Your dress **complements** your blue eyes.

Compose or *Comprise?*

To **compose** means to make up. To **comprise** means to be made up of, or to include.

> **Examples:** Six states **compose** New England.
>
> New England is **composed** of six states.
>
> New England **comprises** six states.

Conscience or *Conscious?*

Tough words to spell, these two!

> **Examples:** A **conscience** makes you feel guilty if you do something wrong.
>
> You can probably do something wrong only if you are **conscious,** or aware!

Continual or *Continuous?*

There is a slight distinction between these two words.

Continual means happening over and over again, usually in rapid succession.

Continuous means steadily, without stopping.

> **Examples:** The three days of **continuous** rain depressed me.
>
> The **continual** hurricanes we are having this year are frightening.

Criteria: Singular or Plural?

Criteria, data, media? Are they singular or plural? Well, they each have singular forms, so technically, these forms are plural. ***Criterion, datum, and medium*** are the singular forms.

However, ***data*** and ***media*** are often thought of as singular and are used with a singular verb. We don't usually use ***medium*** and ***datum***. Not so for ***criteria***. ***Criteria*** should be used with a plural verb. For the singular, use ***criterion,*** and use a singular verb with it.

> ***Examples:***   There ***are three criteria*** for acceptance into the program.
>
> One ***criterion is*** to have a 4.0 grade point average.
>
> The ***data shows*** improved test scores. (***data*** used with a singular verb)
>
> The ***media is*** covering the event. (***media*** used with a singular verb)

Note: How can you tell the difference between the singular and plural forms of the verb? Usually you just know because it sounds right. However, you can always check it out this way: The singular form is the one that sounds right using ***he*** as the subject. The plural form is the one that sounds right using ***they*** as the subject. For example: ***He runs. They run. Runs*** is the singular form of the verb; ***run*** is the plural form.

Some words, such as ***news, physics, economics,*** and ***mathematics,*** sound plural, but are really singular and used with a singular verb.

> ***Examples:***   The news ***is*** good. (not ***are good***)
>
> Mathematics ***is*** my favorite subject. (not ***are my favorite subject***)

Dash or Hyphen? They Are Different

Dashes and hyphens are not the same. In fact, there are three, not two, sizes of these little lines:

-   is a hyphen.

–   is an en dash.

—   is an em dash.

Okay. What are they used for?

A hyphen (-) is made by pressing the key after the zero on your keyboard. It is the shortest of the three lines. Hyphens are used to separate parts of words.

Some compound words use a hyphen: ***self-motivated, mother-in-law***. Most compound words don't use the hyphen any longer: ***email, onsite, website, cooperate, resell***. Sometimes, words start out as two separate words (***web site***). When they become more commonly used, the words are hyphenated (***web-site***), and then become one word (***website***). If you make a compound adjective out of two words, for example, ***book-toting*** boy, the adjective is hyphenated when it comes before the noun it describes, but is not hyphenated when it comes after.

Examples:	He is a ***four-year-old*** boy.
	Stop acting like a ***four year old***.
	This is a ***gas-guzzling*** car.
	The car is ***gas guzzling***.

If you don't know whether or not to hyphenate a word, you can look it up. However, you will often find that different sources disagree. If this is the case, choose one way of writing the word, and write it that way consistently.

Hyphens are also used to separate a word at the end of the line when the entire word cannot fit on one line. Because of computers, this use of hyphens is now much less common. If you are writing by hand and separate a word at the end of a line, remember that you must separate the word at the syllable break, you cannot ever divide a one-syllable word, and you cannot separate a word so that one letter stands by itself on a line.

An en dash (–) is made by pressing Shift and the hyphen on the numeric pad of your keyboard simultaneously. If you type two hyphens in a row, the computer will sometimes make them into an en dash for you. En dashes have two common uses:

- An en dash is used to make a minus sign or negative sign in math.

- An en dash is used to make number ranges in text or in an index. There should be no space before or after the dash.

An em dash (—) is made by pressing Control, Alt, and the hyphen on the numeric pad of your keyboard simultaneously. Note that there is no space before or after an em dash.

Many people just use an en dash instead of an em dash because it is easier to make. Is that correct? Well, not really.

Em dashes are the dashes you use to indicate a big break of thought in sentences. There really isn't much place for em dashes in formal writing, however; they are more casual. In formal writing, you can probably substitute parentheses where you might want to put dashes.

> ***Example:***   I bought a new bowl—I wish I had thought of it before the party—for serving salad.

You can check to make sure your dashes are placed correctly. When you take out the words within the dashes, the sentence should still make sense grammatically. You could put those words in parentheses instead. However, commas **cannot** always be used instead of dashes, because often the words between the dashes make up a complete sentence. You cannot put commas around a complete sentence within a sentence.

Dashes or Parentheses?

Both dashes and parentheses are used to include nonessential elements in a sentence. These elements provide additional information and could be left out of the sentence. Many times the dash and parentheses are interchangeable. Here, however, are two points to consider:

A dash is more informal and probably should not be used in business writing.

A dash is used for a larger break in thought and to provide more emphasis than parentheses.

Examples: My dog—I couldn't believe it—found its way home from three miles away!

My dog (a rescued Chihuahua) found her way home from the park.

Dates: How Do I Write Them?

Here are some rules for writing dates:

1. When you use the month/day/year format, always use a comma between the day and year, and always use a comma after the year if the date is in text.

   Example: My sister was born on May, 5, 1999, in Boston.

2. When you use only the month and year in text, do not use a comma between the month and year, or after the year.

   Example: My sister was born in May 1999 in Boston.

3. Write **on the 6ᵗʰ of March** or **on the sixth of March**. However, if the number comes after the month, don't use March sixth. Use March 6 if the number comes after the month.

4.   Use abbreviations for informal memos only.

   Example: 3/6/99

5.   Sometimes you can use expressions such as the **'90s,** but just for informal uses. Also, businesses or schools sometimes use abbreviations such as 2005/06.

5.   There is no apostrophe in expressions such as **the 1990s**. (not **1990's**)

Discrete **or** *Discreet?*

These two words are often confused.

Discreet means able to keep a secret.

   Example: Please be **discreet** about this private situation.

Discrete means separate.

   Example: Please divide the papers into three **discrete** piles.

Disinterested **or** *Uninterested?*

Disinterested means you are impartial and have no interest in whether something goes one way or the other.

Uninterested means you are just not interested in something; you are bored.

   Examples: We need judges who are **disinterested** in the outcome.

   I am **uninterested** in most sports; I would rather go to a museum.

Dived or *Dove?*

You choose. Either form of the past tense of **dive** is okay. Just be consistent if you use the word more than once in the same piece of writing.

Dual or Duel?

Dual means two.

> **Example:** This tool is **dual** purpose. (It has two purposes.)

A **duel** is a fight between two people (usually with guns in the Wild West).

e.g. or *i.e.?*

These two Latin abbreviations mean entirely different things, so know the difference. Sometimes they may be interchangeable, but not always. Since it is best to avoid using these abbreviations in formal writing, you won't have a problem. Just spell them out. Use **for example** and **that is** instead.

e.g. (**exempli gratia** in Latin) means **for example**. However, it is generally best to just use **for example** in formal writing, rather than the abbreviation. If you do use the abbreviation, be sure to put periods after each of the letters, and use commas before and after the abbreviation.

> **Example:** She brought all her painting supplies, **e.g.,** easel, turpentine, and cloths.

i.e. (**id est** in Latin) means **that is**. Once again, it is best to avoid the abbreviation, and just say **that is**. If you do use the abbreviation, put a period after each of the letters and set the abbreviation off with commas.

> **Example:**　He is the drum major, **i.e.,** the leader of the school's marching band.

Earth or earth?

Should earth be capitalized? Mars and Jupiter are.

In general, **earth** is not capitalized. However, if you are using it in a sentence or passage with other heavenly bodies that are generally capitalized, you can capitalize it for consistency.

> **Examples:**　People used to think that the **earth** was flat.
>
> 　　　　　　The planets closest to **Earth** are Mars and Venus.

Emigrate or Immigrate?

One of these words is coming and one is going.

The prefix **e** or **ex** means **out**. If you **emigrate,** you leave a place.

If you **immigrate**, you go to a place.

> **Examples:**　The family **emigrated from** China to the United States.
>
> 　　　　　　The family **immigrated to** the United States from China.

Eminent or Imminent?

These two words have completely different meanings. Also, note that **imminent** has a double **m**; **eminent** does not.

Eminent means prominent, distinguished.

Imminent means impending, likely to happen without delay.

> **Examples:** He is an ***eminent*** scholar in the field of astronomy.
>
> The dark clouds show that a storm is ***imminent***.

Everyone or *Every One?*

Everyone means everybody, the whole bunch of them.

Every one means every single one of them.

> **Examples:** ***Everyone*** had a really good time at the party.
>
> ***Every one*** of the pizzas was entirely eaten.

Everyone: Singular or Plural?

Everyone sounds like a whole lot of people, right? So should it be plural? Actually, it is singular, and its use can cause problems.

For example, you might say

> ***Everyone is bringing their suitcases***.

Technically, the above sentence is incorrect. Look at the verb. The verb is ***is***, which is singular. (You can tell because you would use ***is*** with ***he,*** and ***he*** is singular. You would use ***are*** with ***they,*** and ***they*** is plural.) If your verb is singular, the subject that goes with it must also be singular. (Refer to the section "Agreement.")

However, notice that you have also used ***their,*** which refers back to ***everyone***. ***Everyone*** is singular (it sounds right with the singular verb you have used), but ***their*** is plural. They don't agree, and they need to.

Well, the choice in the English language is to use ***his or her suitcases,*** and that is really awkward. You could use ***his,*** but that is gender biased. You could switch back and forth between ***his*** and ***her,*** but that is nonsense.

It is best to rewrite and avoid the problem altogether.

> ***Example:***   ***All*** the students ***are bringing their*** suitcases.

Now, everything is plural.

In addition to ***everyone*** being singular, the following pronouns are also singular:

everything, everybody, someone, something, somebody, anyone, anything, anybody, no one, nobody, nothing, one, each, and ***none***.

Exclamation Point–or Not?

Oh, the exclamation mark is such fun to use, especially when you use three or four in a row!!!! Don't!

The exclamation mark can easily be overused. It really has no place at all in formal writing, and it is said that an entire novel should have no more than two exclamation points. So watch your use of this mighty symbol.

Of course, if you are writing to a friend, it is entirely up to you!

Farther or *Further*?

Farther has to do with **distance**.

Further has to do with **additional** or **more**.

> **Examples:** I live **farther** away from the theater than you do.
>
> I cannot discuss this any **further**.

Fewer or Less?

Use **fewer** with items that you can count (generally plural).

Use **less** with items that you cannot count (generally singular).

> **Examples:** There are **fewer books** on this shelf than on the top shelf.
>
> There is **less room** on this shelf for books.
>
> There are **fewer eggs** in this cookie recipe.
>
> There is **less sugar** in this cookie recipe.
>
> I ate **fewer pieces** of pizza than you ate.
>
> I ate **less pizza** than you did.

First or Firstly?

Use **first,** not **firstly**.

You can use **first of all,** but do not use **first off**.

Use **second** and **third,** not **secondly** and **thirdly**; and use **last,** not **lastly**.

> **Examples:** There are three reasons I was late for the party. **First,** I had to stop and get gas for the car. **Second,** I got lost. **Last,** I had trouble finding a parking space.

Notice that these words are followed by a comma when they begin a sentence.

Formally or Formerly?

Formally comes from the word **formal**.

If you are dressed **formally,** you are wearing a tux.

Formerly comes from the word **former**. It means **before now**.

Examples: If you are dressed **formally,** you might be wearing a gown.

I **formerly** lived in Texas, but I live in Florida now.

Former or Latter?

The **former** is the first one, and the **latter** is the second one.

Example: I love both chocolate and vanilla ice cream, the **former** being my favorite. (The **former** would be chocolate, and the **latter** would be vanilla.)

Fractions: Do I Spell Out?
Is There a Hyphen?

Generally, spell out fractions unless doing so would be really complicated (for example, seven sixty-fourths of an inch).

Hyphenate fractions that are used as adjectives directly before a noun.

Examples: I have **two-thirds** box of cookies. (Used directly before **box**)

Two thirds of the box is left.

I ate only **two thirds**.

In the second two examples, two thirds is not placed right before the noun it is describing. You do not need the hyphen.

Fractions that contain whole numbers (3 ½) should generally be written as figures and not spelled out, unless they appear at the beginning of a sentence. You must spell out a number or fraction at the beginning of a sentence.

Examples: Three-and-a-half doughnuts are in that box.

The box contains 3 ½ doughnuts.

Note that in tables and diagrams, fractions are usually not spelled out.

Good or *Well*?

Good is an adjective, and ***well*** is an adverb. Adjectives generally modify or describe nouns, whereas adverbs generally modify or describe verbs.

Examples: I did ***well*** on my test. (***Well*** describes how I ***did,*** which is a verb here, so use ***well***.)

I got a ***good*** grade on my test. (***Good*** describes ***grade,*** which is a noun here, so use ***good***.)

He swims really ***well***.

He is a ***good*** swimmer.

There is (of course) an exception. With verbs of sense, such as ***look, sound, feel, taste,*** you would use the adjective.

Examples: That pizza looks really ***good***.

The music sounds ***good***.

That soft fur feels ***good***.

Chocolate always tastes ***good*** to me.

If someone asks how you are, *I feel good* and *I feel well* are both acceptable. *I feel good* is grammatically correct, but *well* has been accepted as a state of health, so it is fine either way.

Got or Has?

If you obtained something, you *got* it. Once you get it, you *have* it.

Examples: I *got* a new bicycle for my birthday.

I *have* a new bicycle. (Not, I *have got* a new bicycle.)

I don't *have* any money. (Not, I don't *got* any money.)

Hanged or Hung?

Hanged and *hung* are both past tense forms of *hang,* but they are used differently. Hanging a picture is certainly different from hanging a criminal.

Examples: I *hung* the picture in my kitchen.

They *hanged* the man who was convicted of murder.

He or Him? (And All the Others)

These two forms of the pronoun *he* are often confused. Here is the basic rule:

Use *he* as the subject of a verb. Use *him* for everything else (almost).

At the beginning of a sentence, **he** will almost always be your correct choice.

Examples:	**He** is going to the movies.
	He and I are going to the movies.
	His sister and **he** are going to the movies.

Hint: If there is another person in the sentence, take the other person out, and see if **he** works.

If you take out **his sister,** you have **He is going to the movies**. You wouldn't say **Him is going to the movies,** so you know that **He** is correct.

If **he** is not clearly the subject, it is probably an object. You probably won't run into trouble with this one unless there are two objects. Just take the other person out and see if **him** makes sense.

Examples:	I made **him** a birthday cake.
	I made **him and her** a birthday cake.
	They gave a gift to **him and me**.

If you take the other person out in the above examples, you have ***I made him a birthday cake*** and ***They gave a gift to him***. Those are correct.

The other personal pronouns work the same way. Here are the pronouns you use for subjects:

I, we, he, she, they, who (***you*** is always ***you***)

Here are the pronouns you use for objects (not subjects) of a verb:

me, us, him, her, them, whom (***you*** is always ***you***)

Here are some examples of pronouns used correctly.

Examples:	**We** team members won the first game. (Take out ***team members*** to know for sure.)

They gave the prize to **us** team members. (Take out **team members** to know for sure.)

Between **you and me,** I think she is lying. (Never say **between you and I**. It is wrong.)

I divided the pie between **her and him**. (**I** is the subject of the verb **divided**. Therefore, **her** and **him** are not subjects. (They are objects of the preposition **between**.) Therefore, do not use **he** or **she**.)

They and **I** are packing for China today. (**They** and **I** are the subjects of the verb **are packing**.)

Of course, there is an exception to the rule! If you are using the **to be** verb (**am, are, is, was, were, will be**) without another verb, use the subject form in formal English.

Examples:　　Yes, this is **she**.

It is **I**. (In informal conversation, however, you can say **It's me**.)

Healthful or Healthy?

Healthful means promoting good health. Therefore, some foods are actually **healthful,** not **healthy**.

Healthy means having good health.

Examples:　　Vegetables are **healthful** foods.

That is a very **healthy** baby!

His or Her, or Their?

Refer back to the section "Everyone: Singular or Plural" for more help with this one.

Basically, you want to avoid using ***his or her*** because it is awkward. However, to use ***their*** instead is incorrect. So what do you do?

Everyone is wearing their costumes. This sentence is incorrect. The verb ***is*** is singular, and is used with a singular subject. For example, you would say ***he is,*** not ***they is***. Well, ***everyone*** is singular too, since the subject and verb must match: either both singular or both plural. ***Their*** refers back to everyone, so it must be singular as well. However, ***their*** is plural. If you don't want to use ***his or her costume,*** the best thing to do is make the subject and verb plural, so you can then say ***their costumes*** and you will be correct.

> **Example:**   ***All*** the guests ***are wearing their*** costumes.

Now, everything is plural and matches just fine.

You can use ***his or her***. It isn't wrong; it is just a little awkward. I wouldn't recommend using just ***him,*** unless you know everyone is male. And I wouldn't alternate between ***him*** and ***her***. That is just weird and confusing.

I Could Care Less?

No. The correct way to say this one is ***I couldn't care less***.

I could care less doesn't make any sense. If you **could** care less, why use the expression at all?

I or Me? (We or Us?)

Got this one covered. Refer to the section "He or Him? (And All the Others)" for the lowdown on this topic.

If or Whether?

If is often used when **whether** is the correct choice. **If** is conditional. **Whether** is a choice. (When followed by ...**or not,** always use **whether**.)

Examples: I don't know **whether** to go or to stay home.

Whether or not you decide to join me, I will still go.

I don't know **whether** to study tonight.

If it rains, we can't go.

I will go **if** I can find the money.

I will go **if** my sister goes.

Imply or Infer?

These two words are actually opposites. **Imply** goes in one direction, and **infer** goes in the other. To **imply** is to suggest something without coming out and saying it directly. You can **imply** with words, or even gestures or facial expressions.

To **infer** is to assume that something is true from the information you have.

I might **imply** that I got a great grade on my test by something I say or by the smile on my face. And although I didn't come right out and say I got a great grade, you **infer** it from something that I say or from the expression on my face.

Imply goes out, and **infer** comes in.

> **Examples:** The big smile on her face **implied** she was happy about something.
>
> I **inferred** she was happy when I saw the big smile on her face.

Into or *In To?*

Important distinction here. Check out these examples:

> **Examples:** I turned my book **in to** the library. (Correct)
>
> I turned my book **into** the library. (Magician, maybe?)

Into as one word (a preposition) answers the question **Where?**

In to as separate words doesn't answer **Where?** The **in** is actually an adverb that goes with the verb, and the **to** goes with the words that follow it. If you use **in to** properly, you will probably pause briefly between the two words.

> **Examples:** I drove my car **into** the garage. (where?)
>
> I turned my paperwork in to the office. (turned my paperwork **in**.)
>
> I went **into** the store. (where?)
>
> I went **in to** see if I could find a new dress. (**in** goes with **went**; **to** goes with **see**.)

It's I or *It's Me?*

Technically, *it's I* is correct. Refer back to the section "He or Him? (And All the Others)" for the reasons why. In conversation, it is fine to say, *it is me*. However, in formal writing, use *it is I*. Also use *it is she, it is he, this is she, it is they,* etc.

It's or *Its?*

This confusion has been around for a long time. *It's* with the apostrophe (') is a contraction meaning *it is*. *Its* without the apostrophe is the possessive of *it* and implies ownership.

Examples: *It's* raining outside. (*It is* raining outside.)

The cat is eating *its* food. (The food belongs to the cat. If you substitute *it is* in here, it wouldn't make any sense.)

How can you remember this? Well, **all** contractions have an apostrophe (*it's, don't, can't, he's,* etc.). However, **no** possessive pronouns have an apostrophe *(its, ours, yours, hers, his, theirs)*. *It's* and *its* follow that rule.

Italics?

There are several uses for italics. Remember that if you are writing by hand (does anyone do that anymore?), you cannot write in italics, no matter how hard you try. In handwriting, underline to indicate italics.

Here are some rules for using italics:

1. Use italics when you refer to a word or a letter as itself in your writing.

   Examples: You used too many **and's** in this sentence. (Notice that when you made the word plural, you used an **apostrophe** and an **s**. That **s** is **not** in italics.)

          Do you know the meaning of the word **surreptitious**?

          I got all **A's** on my report card.

2. Use italics for foreign words that are not usual words in the English language.

   Many foreign words have been used often enough (for example, **status quo, joie de vivre, chutzpah**) that they don't need italics.

3. Use italics for specific names of boats, trains, and aircraft. Don't use italics for the brand, just for a specific name.

   Examples: **The Spirit of St. Louis** is a famous plane.

          His yacht, **Marge,** is named after his wife.

          He took a cruise on the **Britannica**.

   (Note that sometimes **the** is part of a name and other times, it isn't.)

4. Use italics for titles of books, movies, TV shows, albums or CDs, works of art, and operas. However, use quotation marks for parts of those works: book chapters, episodes of television shows, song titles, etc.

   Examples: I just read **To Kill a Mockingbird** for the first time.

          Turn to the chapter titled "Ancient Rome" in your history book.

          I saw **Star Wars** six times.

          I always watch **Six Abbey Place** on television.

I really enjoyed the episode called "The Bumpetts Go on Vacation."

Will you play the **The Kinks Greatest Hits** for me?

I cry when I listen to "But Now You're Gone."

Lead or *Led?*

Let's say that today I am going to *lead* the parade. The past tense of *lead* is *led*.

Example: Last year I *led* the parade.

The only *lead* that is pronounced *led* is the *lead* in your pencil.

Example: This box is as heavy as *lead*.

Last year I *led* the parade.

The words *lead* and *led* in the examples are pronounced the same, but are spelled differently.

Lend or *Loan?*

Yes, there is a difference! They are different parts of speech.

Lend is a verb. It is an action. You *lend* something to someone.

Loan is not a verb; it is a noun, a thing. So you can't *loan* something to someone. You can, however, *make a loan* to someone.

And the past tense of *lend* is *lent,* just like *send* and *sent*.

Examples: I *lent* him $100 to pay his rent.

I hope he pays back the *loan* I gave him.

Libel or *Slander?*

You don't want to be accused of doing either of these things, but they are different and can be confused.

Libel is **printing** something that damages someone's reputation.

Slander is **saying** something that damages someone's reputation.

Lie or *Lay?*

This one is a really common confusion! The difference between these two verbs, grammatically, is that *lie* is an intransitive verb (has no direct object) and *lay* is a transitive verb (has a direct object).

In other words, you must *lay* something. Here are some examples to clarify this usage:

Examples:	I am going to *lie* in the sun today.
	I am going to *lay my blanket* in the sun. (*lay* the blanket)
	The dog is *lying* by the door.
	The men are *laying tile* in the bathroom. (*laying* tile)
	Can you *lie* on the other lounge chair, please?
	Can you *lay your jacket* on the chair, please? (*lay* your jacket)

As if this weren't all confusing enough, it is the past tense that really makes things confusing, because the past tense of *lie* is *lay*! The past tense of *lay* is *laid*.

Examples:	Yesterday, I *lay* in the sun all afternoon.
	I *laid my blanket* in the sun this morning.

Last night the dog *lay* by the door to keep cool.

Yesterday, the men *laid tile* in the bathroom.

The past participle form of *lie* is *lain*. The past participle of *lay* is, once again, *laid*. The past participle is the form of the verb you would use with *have* or *had*.

Examples: Every day this week I have *lain* in the sun for hours.

I have *laid* my blanket in the same spot all week.

The dog has *lain* by the door every night this week.

The men have *laid* tile for me before.

So, to sum it all up:

Present	Past	Past Participle
lie	lay	have lain
lay	laid	have laid

Loose or Lose?

My pants will be too *loose* if I *lose* weight.

If your cat gets *loose* or your pants are *loose,* you pronounce the *s* as usual. And don't forget the double *o*.

To *lose* something is to not be able to find it, and the *s* is pronounced like a *z*.

Many or *Much?*

Many and *much* are similar to *few* and *less*.

Many is used with things you can count (generally plural).

Much is used with things you cannot count (generally singular).

Examples: I don't have *many* pencils. (not *much* pencils)

I don't have *much* paper.

I don't have *many* pieces of paper. (pieces can be counted)

May or *Might?*

It is usually pretty easy to figure out the difference and similarity between these two words. *May* implies permission, but can also imply possibility. *Might* expresses possibility.

Examples: You *may* leave the room for a few minutes. (permission)

You *might* be asked to give a speech. (possibility)

You *may* be asked to make a speech. (possibility)

However, in the past tense, there is a shade of difference in their uses. Use *may* for a possibility in which you don't know the outcome. Use *might* for a possibility that ultimately didn't happen, but could have. The examples will make this clearer.

Examples: He *may* have been injured. (Possible, but we don't know for sure.)

He *might* have been injured if we didn't catch him. (He could have been, but he wasn't.)

Me or Myself?

Myself and all the other pronouns that end in *-self (yourself, itself, herself, himself, ourselves, themselves)* are called **intensive** or **reflexive** pronouns. They either intensify what has been said or reflect another pronoun in the sentence.

Here is the rule:

Don't use *myself* in a sentence unless "*I*" is the subject.

Don't use *himself, herself,* or *itself* in a sentence unless the subject is *he, she,* or *it*.

Don't use *ourselves* in a sentence unless the subject is *we*.

Don't use *themselves* in a sentence unless the subject is *they*.

> *Examples:* (Notice how the pronouns match.)
>
> > *I myself* am going to make the presentation, not my assistant.
> >
> > *I* made that basket *myself*.
> >
> > *She* learned how to speak Spanish by *herself*.
> >
> > The *actor himself* took a picture with me.
> >
> > *You* should do this *yourself*.
> >
> > *They* cannot go across the street by *themselves*.
> >
> > *They* helped *themselves* to the candy.

Examples of incorrect use:

> > *He* gave the candy to my brother and *myself*.
> >
> > Should be: He gave the candy to my brother and *me*.
> >
> > They wanted to bring my brothers and *myself* along.
> >
> > Should be: They wanted to bring my brothers and *me* along.

Misplaced Modifier?

A **modifier** describes something in a sentence. A modifier can be an adjective describing a noun (***blue*** dress) or an adverb describing a verb (walked ***slowly***).

> **Examples:** I baked a ***cake with chocolate frosting***. (The prepositional phrase ***with chocolate frosting*** describes ***the cake***.)
>
> ***Wearing a silly grin, I*** did a back flip. (The participial phrase ***wearing a silly grin*** describes ***I***.)
>
> ***Seated in the corner, the girl*** didn't say anything. (The participial phrase ***seated in the corner*** describes ***the girl***.)

Notice that the modifiers are placed near the word they modify. In the English language, we assume that words go with the words they are nearest to. Thus, it is important to put your modifiers in the right place. If you don't, your writing may be unclear. Worse than that, it may be downright silly. Here are some mistakes in placing modifiers (misplaced modifiers).

> ***Examples*** of misplaced modifiers:
>
> Incorrect: I went to the dance ***wearing my best dress***. (While this is probably understandable to the reader, it actually says that the dance is wearing the dress.)
>
> Better: ***Wearing my best dress, I*** went to the dance.
>
> Incorrect: She walked her ***dog wearing workout clothes***. (Was the dog wearing the workout clothes?)
>
> Better: While she was ***wearing her workout clothes,*** she walked the dog.

Incorrect: ***While still in diapers, my mother*** went to the Olympics. (Huh?? This sentence simply needs a word added, but it is easy to make a mistake like this.)

Better: ***While I was still in diapers,*** my mother went to the Olympics.

Incorrect: I just bought an antique desk suitable for ***a writer with large drawers and thick legs***. (Did the writer have large drawers and thick legs?)

Better: I just bought an antique desk with large drawers and thick legs; it is suitable for a writer.

Incorrect: ***Growling loudly, I*** fed my hungry dog. (Who is growling?)

Better: I fed my hungry dog because ***he was growling***.

Incorrect: ***Reading a mystery novel by the window, my cat*** sat in my lap. (Smart cat?)

Better: My cat sat in my lap as ***I was reading a mystery novel*** by the window.

Note that there are usually many ways to correct a sentence. You can turn the words around, add words, subtract words, make two sentences, etc.

More Important or More Importantly?

More important means *"what is more important."* ***More importantly*** means *"in a more important way."*

Examples: ***More important,*** we should save the school from closing.

He treated dogs ***more importantly*** than people.

News: Singular or Plural?

Some words look plural (they have an **s** at the end, and if you take away the **s**, you still have a word), but are actually singular. You would use a singular verb with words such as these:

news, mathematics, physics, economics, headquarters

Examples: The **news is** good. (not **are good**)

Mathematics is my favorite subject. (not **are**)

Other words are plural, but don't look plural. Some we consider singular, and some we consider plural.

Two of the common examples are ***criteria*** and ***data***.

Data is actually plural (the singular is ***datum***). However, we hardly ever see the word ***datum*** used, and we generally use a singular verb with data, even though it is technically plural.

Example: The ***data shows*** that protein is good for you. Not the ***data show***.

Criteria is also plural and, unlike ***data, criteria*** should be used with a plural verb. The singular form of ***criteria*** is ***criterion,*** which should be used with a singular verb.

Examples: The only ***criterion*** to qualify for this game ***is*** honesty.

The ***criteria*** we are looking for on your resume ***are*** a college degree and previous experience.

None Is or *None Are?*

Tricky one here. **None** is technically a singular pronoun. However, it can be either singular or plural, depending upon the noun it refers to.

Examples: **None of the children are** coming with us. (plural, to agree with **children**)

                       None of the pie is left. (singular, to agree with **pie**)

                       None of the crayons are in the box. (plural, to agree with **crayons**)

If you can count what **none** refers to, use it as a plural; otherwise, use it as a singular.

Examples: **None** of the **pencils are** left.

                       None of the **sugar is** on the floor.

If you use **not one,** instead of **none,** you would always use a singular verb.

Examples: **Not one** of the children **is** going.

                       Not one of the pencils **is** left.

Numbers: When Do I Spell Them Out?

Here are some general rules for spelling out numbers:

1. Numbers are generally not spelled out in tables.

2. In text for more technical or business materials, numbers **one** through **ten** are spelled out; numbers above **ten** are expressed as numerals.

3. In more formal (more literary) and less technical writing, numbers up to 100 should be spelled out. Numbers ***twenty-one*** through ***ninety-nine*** are hyphenated.

4. Numbers above 100 that can be expressed in one or two words should also be spelled out (***two thousand, one million***).

5. Ordinals (***first, second, third,*** etc.) should be spelled out.

6. Never use a numeral to begin a sentence. Either spell out the number or rewrite the sentence so that the number doesn't come first:

    Example: No: 321 guests attended the event.

                   Yes: There were 321 guests at the event.

7. If you have numbers both above and below 100 that refer to the same thing, either spell them out or use numbers, but be consistent.

    Example: There are 145 boys and 97 girls on the team.

Only: Where Do I Put It?

Only is a very versatile word. Look at these sentences.

Examples: ***Only*** she ate pizza with anchovies. (No one else ate pizza with anchovies.)

               She ***only*** ate pizza with anchovies. (Technically means she ate it and didn't do anything else with it.)

               She ate ***only*** pizza with anchovies. (She didn't eat anything else.)

               She ate pizza ***only*** with anchovies. (Not unless it had anchovies.)

She ate pizza with **only** anchovies. (Nothing else on it.)

Usually, the placement of **only** does not lead to confusion, but the word is often put in an incorrect place. **Only** should be put closest to the word it describes.

Examples: Often said: She **only ate pizza** with anchovies.

Clearer: She ate pizza **only with anchovies**.

Often said: **I only got three wrong** on the exam.

Clearer: **I got only three wrong** on the exam. (**Only** goes with **three**, not **got**.)

A similar situation occurs with the word **almost**.

Examples: Often said: I **almost** ran three miles. (You may not have run at all. You **almost** ran.)

Clearer: I ran **almost three miles**. (You ran two and a half miles, maybe?)

Parallel Construction: What Is It?

Parallel construction means using the same grammatical construction for similar items in a sentence.

Examples: Not parallel: I like to **run, swim,** and **playing** golf.

Parallel: I like to **run, swim,** and **play** golf.

Not parallel: We **shopped** in Paris, **went** sightseeing in London, and **to visit** friends in Rome. (**Shopped** and **went** match, but **to visit** doesn't.)

Parallel: We **went** shopping in Paris, **did** some sightseeing in London, and **visited** some friends in Rome. (**Went, did,** and **visited** all match.)

Lists should also be parallel in construction.

The list below is not parallel.

Example: You will get these benefits from the class:

- Learn new software

- Be able to install the software

- Complete a spreadsheet

- You will know how to troubleshoot the software

- Make connections in your industry

The list below is parallel.

Example: You will get these benefits from the class:

- Learn new software

- Be able to install the software

- Complete a spreadsheet

- Learn how to troubleshoot the software

- Make connections in your industry

In the first list, one item is a complete sentence. (You will know how to troubleshoot the software.) Thus, the list is not parallel. The list should have either all complete sentences or no complete sentences.

Parentheses (and Brackets): How and When?

Parentheses ( ) are used to enclose additional, and often less important or unnecessary, information. In less formal writing, such information is sometimes enclosed with em dashes (—). Sometimes commas may be used to enclose such information, but only if the information is not a complete sentence.

Examples: Mr. Franklin *(my distant cousin)* won an award for his research.

Mr. Franklin—*a distant cousin*—won an award for his research.

Mr. Franklin, *a distant cousin,* won an award for his research.

Any of the above examples will do. However, sometimes in formal writing, you will want to use parentheses rather than dashes.

Examples: *The new movie (it has been rated X) is not appropriate for children*. You cannot use commas here because you cannot enclose a complete sentence with commas. You could also write that sentence like this:

The new movie is not appropriate for children. (It has been rated X.) In this case, you probably wouldn't really need to put the second sentence in parentheses at all, but if you did, it would be punctuated as a regular sentence with a capital letter and a period. The period for the first sentence would be before the parentheses. However, this would also be correct: *The new movie is not appropriate for children (it has been rated X).*

Here are some correct uses of parentheses:

Examples: Mr. Franklin (1923–1999) was my uncle.

Mr. Franklin (a distant cousin) emigrated from Germany.

Mr. Franklin emigrated from Germany. (He is a distant cousin of mine.)

Turn to Chapter 7 (page 235) in your textbook.

Do the exercises (A and B) on page 235.

Do the exercises on page 235 (please use a pencil).

What About Brackets?

Brackets [ ] have two common uses:

The first use is for parentheses inside parentheses. You cannot put parentheses inside other parentheses, so you use brackets inside the parentheses; it is not the other way around.

Example: Please do the third example (page 250 [example G] in your textbook).

The second use of brackets is to enclose explanatory information inside a quote. For example, if a newspaper is quoting part of a speech by the mayor and something is unclear to the reader (perhaps because the rest of the speech isn't there), the explanation will be given in brackets. Thus, the words in brackets are not part of the quote.

Example: Mayor Chauncy, in last night's speech, said, "The new construction [the mall on 7th Street] will put our city on the map."

Passed or *Past?*

Passed is the past tense of the verb ***pass***. It implies action.

Past is a preposition.

> **Examples:**   I ***passed*** your house on the way to school.
>
> I went ***past*** your house on my way to school.
>
> Did you ***pass*** the test? I think I ***passed***.
>
> It is ***past*** midnight. The clock has ***passed*** midnight.

Percent and *Percentage*: How Do I Use Them?

Percent is one word. It is generally spelled out, except in tables, where you may use the symbol (**%**). However, do use a numeral with it, even when it is spelled out.

> **Example:**   6 percent

Percent is always used with a number. ***Percentage*** is not. ***Percentage*** can be either singular or plural, depending on the noun to which it refers.

> **Examples:**   A large percentage of the ***money is*** already spent. (Do not use ***percent*** here. Here, ***percentage*** is singular [***money*** is one unit] and the singular verb [***is***] is used.)
>
> A large ***percentage*** of the ***books have*** been sold. (plural)
>
> A large percentage ***are*** going on to college. (The word ***students*** is implied and is plural, so we use ***are,*** the plural verb.

Period or Semicolon?

Both the period and the semicolon can be used to separate two sentences. Remember that a **comma** cannot be used between two sentences. A comma that is used to separate two sentences results in a **comma splice** or **run-on sentence** and is incorrect!

The semicolon is used when the sentences are closely related. Otherwise, use a period between sentences. When you use a semicolon, the first word of the second sentence is not capitalized. Think of a semicolon as taking the place of both a comma and a conjunction **(and, but, so,** etc.)

Examples: I am going shopping; my sister is going to the movies.

(OK to use semicolon. You could also say **I am going shopping, but my sister is going to the movies**.)

My sister and I will be traveling to France for the summer. We have relatives who live there, so we won't need to pay for hotels. (This is probably not the place for a semicolon because the sentences are not that closely related. However, it would not be wrong to use a semicolon.)

It is never wrong to use a period. You don't need to use a semicolon, even if the sentences are related.

It is rare to connect more than two sentences in a row with semicolons and is not recommended.

Possessives: Do I Have It Right?

Possessives imply ownership: **My sister's cat** means **the cat of my sister**. Here are some rules for forming and using possessives:

1. Form the possessive of a singular noun by adding an **apostrophe** and an **s** ('s):

    girl's dress, child's toy, book's title, Mary's dog, dog's tail

2. Form the possessive of a plural noun that doesn't end in **s** by adding an **apostrophe** and an **s**:

    women's department, men's suits, children's playroom

3. Form the possessive of a plural noun that ends in **s** by adding only an **apostrophe**:

    sisters' bicycles (more than one sister), dogs' crates, schools' test scores

4. Form the possessive of a singular noun that already ends in s by adding an **apostrophe** and an **s** (yes, this is correct). You can usually go by the pronunciation:

    boss's schedule, James's book, Mrs. Douglass's glasses

Note that Moses and Jesus add just an **apostrophe** and no **s** for the possessive. Words ending in **es** with an **ez** sound also add just an apostrophe (Xerxes').

5. For plurals of words ending in **s**, go by the pronunciation:

    bosses', princesses' —you wouldn't say **bosses's** or **princesses's,** so you don't write them that way.

6. Possessive pronouns **do not** have **apostrophes: yours, theirs, ours, its, hers**

7. To indicate joint ownership, only the last word needs the **apostrophe** and **s**:

    Mom and Dad's house.

8. To indicate separate ownership, both words must be possessive:

    My sister's and brother's passports.

9. Sometimes we use a possessive before a gerund (a verb with an **-ing** ending, which is being used as a noun)

> I love **your singing**. (instead of **you singing**)

> I am pleased about **your graduating** with honors. (instead of **you graduating**)

> I am unhappy about **your constant talking** in class. (instead of **you talking**)

However, notice that there is a difference in meaning between using the possessive and not. Thus, sometimes it is correct to not use the possessive:

> **I love your singing**. But **I hear you singing**.

Precede or Proceed?

These two words are often confused, not only because one begins with **pre-** (which means **before**) and the other with **pro-** (which means **forward**), but also because one ends in **-cede** and the other in **-ceed**.

They are both verbs (action words). To **precede** means to come before something else. To **proceed** means to continue on.

Examples: The football game will **precede** our Christmas dinner. (The game will come before dinner.)

The parade will **proceed** down Main Street. (The parade will go down Main Street.)

The rainbow was **preceded** by a hailstorm. (The hailstorm came before the rainbow.)

After you left the library, I **proceeded** with my studying. (I continued on with my studying.)

Preposition Problems?

Which preposition to use can sometimes be confusing, particularly for those whose first language is not English. Here are some of the more common issues:

- Use different *from*, not different *than*.

- You graduate *from* high school or college; you don't just graduate high school or college. Don't leave out the *from*.

- Use equal *to,* not equal *with*.

- Use preferable *to,* not preferable *than*.

- Use *inside,* not *inside of* (*inside* the box, not *inside of* the box). Same with *outside*.

- Use *off,* not *off of* (*off the* table, not *off of* the table).

- Use *visit,* not *visit with* (*I visited* Grandma, not *I visited with* Grandma).

- Use just *considered* or *considered to be,* not *considered as*. (It is *considered to be* the best restaurant in town or It is *considered* the best restaurant in town. Do not say It is *considered as* the best restaurant in town.)

- Use *regarded as,* not *regarded as being*. (It is *regarded as* the best place in town. Do not say It is *regarded as being* the best place in town.)

- Sometimes you need different prepositions to go with different words. He *swam in* and *skied on* that lake every year. Don't just say *He swam and skied in that lake every year* if separate prepositions for each verb will make the meaning clearer.

Pronoun Switching?

When you start using a pronoun, stick with that same pronoun to refer to the same person or people. For example, if you are writing in the first person (using the pronoun *I*), don't suddenly start using *you* instead.

> **Example:**   *I* really love dancing. When *I* dance, *I* feel as if *I* can fly. *I* have studied dance for more than ten years. When *you* study dance, *you* must practice every day. *I* am often too tired to practice, but *you* must do it anyway.

In the above example, the writer switches between *I* and *you*. The writer is referring to himself or herself and should stick to the pronoun *I*.

Another common pronoun switch is from *I* or *you* to *one*.

> **Example:**   *I* really love dancing. When *I* dance, *I* feel as if *I* can fly. *I* have studied dance for more than ten years. When *one* studies dance, *you* must practice every day. *I* am often too tired to practice, but *one* must do it anyway.

In the above example, the writer has switched around from *I* to *one* to *you*. This switching around can get confusing and annoying for the reader. Be consistent in pronoun use.

Quotation Marks:
When and Where?

Of course, the most common use of quotations marks is to enclose the exact words someone said. Be sure, however, you don't quote something that is not a direct quote.

Examples: Direct quote: She said, "I think it is going to rain later."

Indirect quote: She said that it is going to rain later.

Here are some things to remember when you use quotation marks for quoting someone's exact words:

1.   Periods and commas always go inside quotation marks. Always.

2.   Semicolons always go outside quotation marks.

3.   Question marks and exclamation marks can go either inside or outside quotation marks. If the question is part of the quote, the question mark goes inside the quotation marks. If the entire sentence is a question, but not the part in quotes, the question mark goes outside. If both the sentence and the quote are questions, put the question mark before the quote. Don't ever use two question marks in a row.

Examples of Using Quotation Marks:

She said, "It is cold out here."

"It is cold out here," she said. "I am going inside."

"It is cold out here," she said, "and I am going inside."

"Are you cold?" she asked.

Did she say, "I am too cold out here"?

Did she ask, "Is anyone else cold?"

4. If the introduction to a quote is long and is a complete sentence, you can use a colon to introduce it rather than just a comma.

   Example: John F. Kennedy spoke these words that we will always remember: "Ask not what your country can do for you; ask what you can do for your country."

5. For quotes that are longer than one paragraph, use beginning quotes in every paragraph, but do not use closing quotes for any of the paragraphs except the last one.

Other Uses for Quotation Marks

You can use quotation marks to enclose something said in sarcasm.

Example: Oh, he is definitely the "best student" in the class!

You can use quotation marks around a slang or colloquial expression.

Example: Well, that makes me "laugh out loud."

You can use quotation marks around words that play an unusual part in a sentence.

Example: She has a real "can-do" attitude.

Finally, quotes are used around titles of short stories, songs, magazine and newspaper articles, and book chapter titles. Refer to the section "Titles: Italics or Quotes?"

Redundancy: Am I Repeating Myself?

Watch out for redundancies in your writing. We all make these slipups without even noticing. Be careful, and always proofread your writing. Here are some redundancies:

6 p.m. at night

as yet (just use **yet**)

at this point in time (use **now**)

close proximity

collaborate together

consensus of opinion (**consensus** is enough)

cooperate together

due to the fact that (use **because**)

for the purpose of (use **for** or **to**)

I have a friend of mine who (**I have a friend who** is enough)

I know the fact that (**I know** is enough)

if and when

in relation to (use **about**)

in the event that (use **if**)

in the immediate vicinity of (use **near**)

inside of (**inside** is enough)

long, long time ago

made a promise (use **promised**)

new innovation

reason is because

small in size

such as, etc. (don't need the **such as**)

the reason is ... is (I keep hearing people repeat the **is**)

the reason why (**the reason** is enough)

true fact

very, very expensive

with regard to (use **about**)

Regretful or *Regrettable?*

If you do something you feel sorry about, you are **regretful,** or full of regret. You can be **regretful,** but you cannot be **regrettable**. **Regrettable** is used for situations that are unfortunate.

Examples: I am **regretful** that I never said goodbye to her.

It is **regrettable** that she had to return to her own country so soon.

Respectfully or *Respectively?*

Respectfully means **with respect**. **Respectively** means **in that order**.

Examples: The boy listened **respectfully** as his father explained what he had done wrong.

I gave the speech to the department and to the boss, **respectively**. (First, I gave the speech to the department, and then I gave the speech to the boss.)

Notice that **respectively** is preceded by a comma.

Say or *Tell?*

There isn't a lot of difference between **say** and **tell**. **Say** generally focuses on the act of speaking, whereas **tell** focuses on the giving of information.

Examples: Please **tell** me a story. (focus on information)

Did you **say** something? (focus on speaking)

I hope you **tell** me the truth. (focus on information)

I didn't **say** anything during the discussion. (focus on speaking)

Did you **tell** her a secret? (focus on information)

Sentence or Fragment?

A sentence is a complete thought. A sentence fragment is not.

Sentence: I threw the ball.

Fragment: Because I threw the ball.

The fragment begs the question,"What happened because you threw the ball?" It is not a complete thought. Many fragments begin with words such as **because, although, when,** and other **subordinating conjunctions** that are meant to begin clauses within sentences.

Notice that you need to add an entire sentence to the fragment **Because I threw the ball** in order to make it a complete thought:

Because I threw the ball, I broke the window.

I broke the window is a complete sentence by itself, and when you add it to the fragment **Because I threw the ball,** you have a more detailed sentence.

Make sure you don't use fragments and call them sentences by putting periods at the end of them.

There is an exception to this rule: You might notice that there are sentence fragments in this book. There are also sentence fragments in most novels you read. Often, in fiction and even creative nonfiction, writers use fragments for effect. This is fine, as long as the writer is doing it on purpose.

Short expressions, such as *yes, no,* and *of course* can be followed by a period and are not really considered fragments.

> **Examples:** I am wondering whether I should say anything. *No.* I am going to keep quiet.
>
> Sue asked me if I wanted to go with her. *Of course.* I wouldn't miss it.

Notice, however, that such expressions are more likely to be used in creative writing.

If you are writing a formal letter, an article, a research paper, or a school essay, don't use any fragments. Write in complete sentences. Formal English requires complete sentences.

Shall or *Will?*

Most of the time, use *will*. *Shall* isn't used very much anymore.

Shall is quite formal and should be used with *I*. Otherwise, use *will*.

> **Examples:** I *shall*.
>
> You *will*.
>
> He, she, it *will*.

However, if you want to show threat or determination, flip it around.

Examples: I **will** go to the dance!

You **shall** clean your room!

She **shall** be punished!

Shined or Shone?

What is the past tense of **shine**? Is it **shone** or **shined**? It is both, depending on how the word is used.

Use **shined** if there is a direct object.

Example: I **shined** my shoes.

Use **shone** if there is no direct object (receiver of the action).

Example: The sun **shone** all day.

Sit or Set?

Refer back to **lie** and **lay** for this one, which is similar.

In grammatical terms, use **sit** if there is no direct object. Use **set** with a direct object.

In other words, you must **set** something. You cannot **sit** something.

Examples: I **sit** on the chair.

I **set my jacket** on the chair.

My dog **sits** on the blanket.

My dog **sets his bone** on the blanket.

Past tense: Yesterday, I **sat** on the chair.

Yesterday, I **set my jacket** on the chair.

Yesterday, my dog **sat** on the blanket.

Yesterday, my dog **set his bone** on the blanket.

Present	Past	Past Participle
sit	sat	have sat
set	set	have set

Sole or Soul?

Both of these words, which are pronounced the same but spelled differently, have two meanings.

Sole is the bottom of your shoe. It also means the **only one**.

Soul is a spiritual entity and also has an idiomatic meaning.

Examples: The **sole** of my shoe is torn, and my feet are getting cold.

Mary was the **sole** survivor of the auto accident.

Some people say murderers have no **soul**.

Please don't tell a **soul** about this.

Oh, and then there is the fish: fillet of **sole**.

Some Time or *Sometimes?*

Sometimes refers to the frequency with which something happens. It means **some of the time**. **Sometime** refers to a specific time. **Some time** refers to an unspecified amount of time.

> **Examples:**   **Sometimes** I take the bus to work.
>
> **Sometime** you will have to come dancing with me. (at some specific time)
>
> I will give you **some time** to think about it. (an unspecified amount of time)

Speak or *Talk?*

There is little difference between these two words, but **speak** is generally more formal. Also, **speak** is usually used for one-way communication, whereas **talk** is used to indicate two-way communication. The two words can usually be used interchangeably and still be correct.

> **Examples:**   He will **speak** in front of the entire company.
>
> I enjoying **talking** on the phone with you.
>
> I would like to **speak** to you about an important matter.
>
> Please do not **talk** to other students during class.

Stationary or *Stationery?*

Stationary with an **-ary** means staying in one place. You can remember which is which by remembering that **place** has an **a** in it, just like the end of **stationary**.

Stationery with an **-ery** is the paper you write letters on—at least before computers came along!

Subjunctive Mood: What's That?

Moods in grammar are associated with verbs. Usually, we use the **subjunctive** mood without even noticing it. The following are examples of the **subjunctive** mood:

Examples:

1. Sometimes the **subjunctive** expresses necessity or demand:

   It is important that she **be** at the graduation. (The usual verb would be **is**.)

   We demanded that he **be** allowed to have the day off.

   It is necessary that he **arrive** on time. (The usual verb would be **arrives**.)

2. Sometimes the **subjunctive** expresses a wish, or something that is not true:

   If I **were** the president of the club, I would do things differently. (The usual verb is **was**.)

   He often told me he wishes he **were** my son. (The usual verb is **was**. Always use subjunctive with **wish**.)

In case you are curious, the other moods in grammar are ***indicative*** (when you are making a statement, which is the most common mood) and ***imperative,*** used for commands.

Such As with Etc.

Do not use ***such as*** and ***etc.*** in a list together. ***Such as*** already implies that there are other items in the list that are not mentioned, so you do not need ***etc.*** there as well.

Examples: Redundant: I would love to visit countries ***such as*** France, Spain, Italy, ***etc.***

Better: I would love to visit countries ***such as*** France, Spain, and Italy.

Also Okay: I would love to visit France, Spain, Italy, ***etc.***

In the above examples, I would use ***such as*** rather than ***etc.***

Swam or Swum?

Lots of verbs (action words) in the English language have irregular forms for the past tense. A regular verb forms its past tense by adding ***-ed*** to the end. Regular verbs include ***walk (walked), play (played), shop (shopped),*** and many, many others.

Irregular verbs form the past tense in other ways. For example, ***think (thought), swim (swam), fight (fought),*** and many others.

There is another verb tense form called the **past participle**. It is the form you use with ***have*** or ***had,*** for example, I ***have walked*** or I ***have thought***. In regular verbs, this form is the same as the past tense.

> ***Example:*** I ***walk,*** I ***walked,*** I ***have walked***.

But sometimes, the present tense (walk), past tense (walked), and past participle (have walked) are all different. Some of them are particularly confusing.

Here are some common, confusing irregular verbs:

> ***Examples:*** I ***swim,*** I ***swam,*** I have ***swum***. (yes, that is correct!)
>
> You ***drink,*** you ***drank,*** you ***have drunk***.
>
> The bell ***rings,*** the bell ***rang,*** the bell ***has rung***.
>
> My shirt ***shrinks,*** my ***shirt shrank,*** my ***shirt has shrunk***.
>
> I ***go,*** I ***went,*** I ***have gone***. (I ***have went*** is incorrect!)
>
> I ***slay,*** I ***slew,*** I ***have slain***.

Than or *Then?*

Than is used in comparisons. ***Then*** refers to time.

> ***Examples:*** I like this color much better ***than*** that one.
>
> I came home, and ***then*** I ate dinner.

Note that you cannot use ***then*** to connect two sentences because it is not a conjunction.

> ***Examples:*** Incorrect: I came home, ***then*** I ate dinner.
>
> Correct: I came home, ***and then*** I ate dinner.

You must use a conjunction (a connecting word such as ***and, but, or, so***) along with ***then***. ***Then*** tells when, and it cannot be used to connect sentences. It is not a conjunction.

That, Which, or Who?

If you are talking about a person, it is always **who**. So that simplifies things a bit.

Examples: I know a woman **who** makes jewelry.

My friend, **who** is going to Africa this summer, is leaving his dog with me.

By the way, animals (even your pet dog) are not considered people, so use **that** and **which** with them.

That leaves **which** and **that**. So when do you use **which,** and when do you use **that**?

Use **which** with commas and **that** when there are no commas.

Examples: I enjoyed the book **that** I just finished.

I liked that book, **which** was written by my favorite author, and I think you will too.

OK. Got it. So when do you use commas? Why are there commas in the second example, but not in the first one?

Words that are set off by a comma (or commas) are considered to be additional information that could be left out without confusing the reader. In the first example, there is no comma because the end of the sentence is needed to help identify the book. In the second example, it is assumed that you know which book is being talked about, and the information inside the commas is more of a "by the way."

Notice that when you say a sentence that needs a comma, you will probably just naturally pause. When you say a sentence that doesn't need a comma, you probably won't pause.

I know **that** he likes me. (You would not pause before **that**.)

My neighbor, **who is from New York,** is moving away. (You would probably pause where the commas are.)

Sometimes a writer will leave out the **that**. Sometimes it is fine to leave it out; but other times, leaving it out confuses the meaning, and it should be left in. To be safe, you can always leave **that** in.

Examples:	I know she is coming for dinner. (This sentence is clear and fine.)
	I know Bob and Henry are coming for dinner. (This sentence would be clearer with **that** left in: I know **that** Bob and Henry are coming for dinner. You would avoid **I know Bob and Henry** being misread.)
	I recommend you listen more carefully. (This sentence would be clearer with **that** left in: I recommend **that** you listen more carefully.)

Their, There, or *They're?*

There, their now ... this one isn't so difficult.

There is a place.

Their belongs to them.

They're is a contraction meaning they are.

Examples:	I saw the spider over **there**.
	There is a spider over **there**.
	I went over to **their** house.
	They're coming over to my house.
	They're looking at **their** new car over **there**.

Titles: How Do I Capitalize?

We know that titles of books, songs, movies, etc., are capitalized, but are all the words capitalized? And if not, which ones aren't? No, not all words in a title are capitalized, but most are. Here are the rules:

1. The first and last words of a title are always capitalized no matter what they are.

2. The articles **a, an,** and **the** are not capitalized unless they are the first or last word.

3. The conjunctions **for, and, nor, but,** and **or,** are not capitalized unless they are the first or last word. (**Yet** and **so** are not capitalized either if they are used as conjunctions, but they are capitalized if they are used as adverbs, which would be likely in a title. See the examples.)

4. Small prepositions of four letters or fewer, such as **up, down, in, our, on, at, to, with, by,** and **for** are not capitalized. Prepositions with more than four letters, such as **among, along, beyond, between,** and others are capitalized.

5. So, to make it easier, remember that any word of five letters or more is going to be capitalized. Most words of two letters are not capitalized.

6. Most important of all: make sure you always capitalize **Is, Am, Are, Was, Were,** and **Be**. These words are verbs and are very important!

    Examples: For Whom the Bell Tolls

    Catcher in the Rye

    I Am the Walrus

    Gone with the Wind

    A Tale of Two Cities

Santa Claus Is Coming to Town

I Love You So Much (**So** is an adverb here, not a conjunction. It tells how much.)

Titles: Italics or Quotes?

Some titles are italicized, and others are enclosed in quotation marks. Remember that if you are writing by hand, you cannot italicize, so you underline instead.

Larger items are generally italicized, and smaller parts of those things are usually enclosed in quotation marks.

In Italics:	**In Quotes:**
Book title	Chapter title or short story
Magazine title	Title of article in a magazine
TV series	Title of one episode in a series
Music CD title	Song title

Names of particular ships, airplanes, trains, and spacecraft are also italicized.

Examples: We watched **Apollo 11** take off.

He named his boat **Marylou** after his wife.

To, Too, or Two?

Two is a number.

Too means **also** or **very**.

To is used the rest of the time. (It is a preposition indicating place, or an infinitive used right before a verb.)

Examples: I have **two** pencils.

I want to go **too**. (Notice that when this type of **too** is at the end of the sentence, there is no comma before it.)

This soup is **too** salty.

Please go **to** school.

I want **to** go shopping.

Toward or *Towards?*

Toward and **towards** are interchangeable, so you choose! Usually, in the United States, we use **toward** without the **s**. In Britain they prefer **towards**.

Uncertainty? Avoid It

Avoid using words that indicate uncertainty in your writing. For example, avoid using **I think** to introduce an idea you are writing about. Other weak and uncertain phrases include **it might, it may, it could**.

Warranty or *Warrantee?*

A **warranty** is some type of guarantee you get with a product to ensure that it will either work or you will get a refund or repair. A **warrantee** is the person to whom the warranty is given.

Who or Whom?

Once and for all, when do you use **who** and when do you use **whom**? Refer back to the "He or Him? (And All the Others)" section for more information; it is the same principle as **who** and **whom**.

In grammatical terms, use **who** for subjects and **whom** for objects. Here are a couple of ways to help you decide which to use.

Find the nearest verb. Figure out who did the action of the verb. If it is the **who** or **whom,** use **who**. If there is another subject (the person or thing that did the action of the verb), use **whom**.

Examples: **Who** is going to the party? (**is going** is the verb, and **who** is doing it.)

Whom did you invite to the party? (**invite** is the verb, **you** invited, so you use **whom**.)

My brother, **who** is graduating this year, wants to become a dentist. (closest verb is **is graduating**, **who** is doing it, so use **who**.)

Another way to figure it out is to substitute **I** or **me,** or **he** or **him**. If **I** or **he** works, use **who**. If **him** or **me** works, use **whom**.

Examples: **Who** is going to the party? (Substitute: **He** is going to the party.)

Whom did you invite to the party? (You invited **him** to the party, so use **whom**.)

My brother, **who** is graduating this year, wants to become a dentist. (**He** is graduating this year, so use **who**.)

- -
Note: Always use **whom** after prepositions such as **by, for,** and **with**.
- -

Writing Tips: Need Some?

Here are some tips to improve your writing:

1. Words have more punch when placed at the end of a sentence.

2. Short words have more punch than long words.

3. After you write, read the words out loud to hear how they sound. This is a good way to pick up mistakes.

4. Always proofread your writing.

5. Always carefully review emails before pressing **Send**. You might even want to type in the person it is going to last, so you don't send something you don't really want to send.

6. Use strong, exact verbs, and you won't need as many adverbs.

   Example: Avoid: He walked back and forth anxiously, waiting for news.

   Better: He paced the floor, waiting for news.

7. Don't confuse the time something happened with the time you are talking about it.

8. Short sentences are stronger and often more effective.

9. Mix long and short sentences, and use a variety of sentence structures.

10. Write in the positive, rather than in the negative.

11. Put correlatives in the right place.

   Example: Incorrect: I neither have milk nor juice in the refrigerator.

   Correct: I have neither milk nor juice in the refrigerator.

12. Don't separate the subject and verb with words that could be at the beginning of the sentence.

    Example: Avoid: She, when she was a child, lived all over Europe.

    Better: When she was a child, she lived all over Europe.

13. Avoid dull words like **good, nice,** and **interesting**.

14. Avoid words like **a lot** (which is two words, not **alot**) and **stuff** and **bunch** (unless you are talking about bananas!).

15. Make sure your reader knows what you are referring to when you use **this** or **it**.

16. Don't start too many sentences with **There is** or **There are**.

17. Remember that spell check doesn't catch everything.

18. Avoid weak verbs like **is** and **has**.

19. Start about two thirds of your sentences with the subject.

20. Don't use compound subjects and compound verbs together; it can be confusing.

    Example: **The boys and the girls sang and danced** at the party.

Your or You're?

Your is the possessive (belongs to you).

You're is the contraction, which means **you are**.

Whenever you mean **you are,** use **you're** (with the apostrophe).

Examples: I assume **you're** coming with us. (you are)

You left **your** coat here.

You're welcome. (you are)

Appendix A
Watch Out for These!

1. ***Irregardless*** is not a word.

2. Don't use ***being as***.

3. Don't use ***being that***.

4. Don't use ***where*** and ***at*** close to each other.

5. Don't use ***in regards to***. Use ***in regard to*** or ***as regards***.

6. If you are writing by hand, don't ever use hearts or circles for dots on your ***i***'s!

7. Don't use ***huh, gonna,*** and other slang and "nonwords."

8. Don't use large fonts when you write business letters or reports. Stay at about 12-point size.

9. Don't ever use color fonts in business writing unless you have a really good reason.

10. Don't use script or other hard-to-read fonts.

11. Don't use company jargon unless your writing is staying within the company.

12. Don't use sarcasm in your writing.

13. Stay away from overused and trite clichés.

14. Avoid sexism in your writing. For example, use ***chairperson*** instead of ***chairman***.

15. Avoid stereotyping in your writing.

16. Spell out symbols such as **%** (percent) and **&** (and).

17. Don't make up words (check the dictionary). If you intentionally make up a word, use quotes around it.

18. Do not plagiarize. It is against the law. Give credit where credit is due.

19. Don't ever use **had ought**.

20. The word is **orient,** not **orientate**.

21. The point is **moot,** not **mute**.

22. Use **about,** rather than **as to**.

23. Height doesn't end in **th,** so don't pronounce it **heighth**!

24. Do not use **and/or**.

25. **Mischievous** doesn't end in **-vious,** so don't pronounce it that way.

26. Avoid using **folks**; it is informal.

27. Avoid using **kind of** and **sort of** in formal writing.

28. Do not use **thank you in advance**.

Index

Contact and Ordering Information

You may order any of my books from my website. They are also available on Amazon, Barnes and Noble, and other online retailers.

If they are not already available as e-books, they will be soon. They will be available for all e-readers and in the iBooks store.

As I write this, *The Best Little Grammar Book Ever!* is available on Nook and Kindle. *Beyond Worksheets* is available as a download from my website.

This book and *The Best Little Grammar Book Ever!* can also be ordered in bulk for your school, association, or company from Ingram Book Company. Contact me for details.

I am available for grammar and business writing workshops at your schoool, business, or organization.

Mailing Address:

> Arlene Miller
> bigwords101
> P.O. Box 4483
> Petaluma, CA 94955

Website: www.bigwords101.com

E-mail: info@bigwords101.com

Telephone: (707) 529-0092